Life Changing Quotes

for

Attitude,
Wisdom
and
Success.

David Sparks

Contents

<u>Introduction</u>

Quotes seem to have a magical quality about them. For some reason, many people love reading them. Maybe its because the words speak to the person or maybe because they like and admire the author. Either way, quotes seem to carry an energy of their own, like a call to action.

Quotes can be inspirational to many, however just as many are not inspired. This may have to do with timing. When a reader reads a quote, they may not be in the appropriate state of mind, or the appropriate stage in their life to appreciate the meaning or lessons behind the words.

As a teacher I have displayed quite a few quotes around my classroom with the hope that one of them will inspire the students and motivate them to work that little bit harder. I was truly amazed when I received a phone call from parents of a student, thanking me for what I had said in class one day. These parents had been having difficulty with their 15-year-old son for quite some time, but he did a turn around after reading one of the new quotes I had put up in the room. The quote was **"time is all you've got and time is running out."** I had heard it while listening to a Jim Rohn tape and thought it would be useful to the students, as school would finish before they knew it.

The quotes written in this book are specifically about Attitude, Wisdom and Success, as I believe, these are three very important areas of life. Our attitude impacts how we see things around us. It colors our perception and makes us either positive or negative about our situation, our family, our work, our friends, the weather, everything.

Wisdom is what we get as a result of living. Too many of today's youth think they have the answers to life even though they are barely out of diapers. They don't realise that it is age and experience that creates wisdom.

Success is a concept which differs for everybody. For some success is attaining something, like reaching a goal or making lots of money. For others it is the process they go through to achieve the goal. Irrespective of one's own beliefs, almost everyone who has lived has achieved success in something, it's just that not everyone can see it.

The words in this book come from actors and actresses, athletes, businessmen and women, politicians, musicians, philosophers, scientists and more. Some quotes go back as far as ancient Rome and ancient Greece and are still relevant to this day.

I suggest this book be used as a regular 'go to', so keep it handy and look at it often. You may read something now which may not resonate with you at this point in your life, but a year or two down the track, it will have a totally different meaning.

You will notice that a few quotes sound the same, but come from different authors. I have put this down to the individuals being on the same wavelength and their experiences having led them to formulate similar beliefs.

Of course, you probably won't find every quote useful or inspiring, but this is to be expected. Since everyone's values are different, different quotations will inspire different people.

Hopefully you will enjoy these quotes for a long time to come and notice the improvements that benefit your life by making the small changes that these sages provoke.

<u>Attitude</u>

Attitude is more important than the past, than education, than money, than circumstances, than what people do or say. It is more important than appearance, giftedness, or skill.

- Charles R. Swindoll

Attitude is a little thing that makes a big difference.

- Winston Churchill

My attitude is that if you push me towards something that you think is a weakness, then I will turn that perceived weakness into a strength.

- Michael Jordan

Weakness of attitude becomes weakness of character.

- Albert Einstein

Your attitude, not your aptitude, will determine your altitude.

- Zig Ziglar

You cannot control what happens to you, but you can control your attitude toward what happens to you, and in that, you will be mastering change rather than allowing it to master you.

- Brian Tracy

Choosing to be positive and having a grateful attitude is going to determine how you're going to live your life.

- Joel Osteen

Your living is determined not so much by what life brings to you as by the attitude you bring to life; not so much by what happens to you as by the way your mind looks at what happens.

- Khalil Gibran

Our environment, the world in which we live and work, is a mirror of our attitudes and expectations.

- Earl Nightingale

Everything can be taken from a man but one thing: the last of human freedoms - to choose one's attitude in any given set of circumstances, to choose one's own way.

- Viktor E. Frankl

Our attitude towards others determines their attitude towards us.

- **Earl Nightingale**

Develop an attitude of gratitude, and give thanks for everything that happens to you, knowing that every step forward is a step toward achieving something bigger and better than your current situation.

- **Brian Tracy**

Nothing can stop the man with the right mental attitude from achieving his goal; nothing on earth can help the man with the wrong mental attitude.

- **Thomas Jefferson**

People may hear your words, but they feel your attitude.

- **John C. Maxwell**

Ability is what you're capable of doing. Motivation determines what you do. Attitude determines how well you do it.

- **Lou Holtz**

Excellence is not a skill. It is an attitude.

- **Ralph Marston**

A positive attitude causes a chain reaction of positive thoughts, events and outcomes. It is a catalyst and it sparks extraordinary results.

- **Wade Boggs**

The greatest day in your life and mine is when we take total responsibility for our attitudes. That's the day we truly grow up.

- **John C. Maxwell**

I hope the millions of people I've touched have the optimism and desire to share their goals and hard work and persevere with a positive attitude.

- **Michael Jordan**

For success, attitude is equally as important as ability.

- **Walter Scott**

If you are going to achieve excellence in big things, you develop the habit in little matters. Excellence is not an exception, it is a prevailing attitude.

- **Colin Powell**

Pink isn't just a color, it's an attitude!

- **Miley Cyrus**

Adopting the right attitude can convert a negative stress into a positive one.

- Hans Selye

A positive attitude can really make dreams come true - it did for me.

- David Bailey

I think whether you're having setbacks or not, the role of a leader is to always display a winning attitude.

- Colin Powell

The remarkable thing is, we have a choice everyday regarding the attitude we will embrace for that day.

- Charles R. Swindoll

Attitude determines the altitude of life.

- Edwin Louis Cole

It is not the body's posture, but the heart's attitude that counts when we pray.

- Billy Graham

Our attitudes control our lives. Attitudes are a secret power working twenty-four hours a day, for good or bad. It is of paramount importance that we know how to harness and control this great force.

- Irving Berlin

Having a positive mental attitude is asking how something can be done rather than saying it can't be done.

- Bo Bennett

Morality is simply the attitude we adopt towards people whom we personally dislike.

- Oscar Wilde

Our lives are not determined by what happens to us but how we react to what happens, not by what life brings us but the attitude we bring to life.

- Wade Boggs

Whenever you're in conflict with someone, there is one factor that can make the difference between damaging your relationship and deepening it. That factor is attitude.

- William James

Watch your manner of speech if you wish to develop a peaceful state of mind. Start each day by affirming peaceful, contented and happy attitudes and your days will tend to be pleasant and successful.

- Norman Vincent Peale

Civilization is a method of living, an attitude of equal respect for all men.

- Jane Addams

The greatest discovery of my generation is that a human being can alter his life by altering his attitudes.

- William James

It is our attitude at the beginning of a difficult task which, more than anything else, will affect its successful outcome.

- William James

Character is the result of two things: mental attitude and the way we spend our time.

- Elbert Hubbard

Attitude is everything.

- Diane von Furstenberg

The attitude is very important. Because, your behavior radiates how you feel.

- **Lou Ferrigno**

There are no menial jobs, only menial attitudes.

- **William J. Brennan, Jr**

The meaning of things lies not in the things themselves, but in our attitude towards them.

- **Antoine de Saint-Exupery**

A complainer is like a Death Eater because there's a suction of negative energy. You can catch a great attitude from great people.

- **Barbara Corcoran**

You cannot tailor-make the situations in life but you can tailor-make the attitudes to fit those situations.

- **Zig Ziglar**

The greatest discovery of my generation is that man can alter his life simply by altering his attitude of mind.

- **James Truslow Adams**

Attitudes are more important than facts.

- George MacDonald

Happiness is an attitude of mind, born of the simple determination to be happy under all outward circumstances.

- J. Donald Walters

Great effort springs naturally from great attitude.

- Pat Riley

There is little difference in people, but that little difference makes a big difference. The little difference is attitude. The big difference is whether it is positive or negative.

- W. Clement Stone

Bad attitudes will ruin your team.

- Terry Bradshaw

Really you just gotta keep chugging along and keep a positive attitude and get through all the problems. You gotta face them, otherwise you don't get through.

- Lesley Gore

Our attitude toward life determines life's attitude towards us.

- John N. Mitchell

When you are thwarted, it is your own attitude that is out of order.

- Meister Eckhart

Time plays a role in almost every decision. And some decisions define your attitude about time.

- John Cale

Funny is an attitude.

- Flip Wilson

The biggest challenge is how to affect public attitudes and make people care.

- Jim Fowler

Stop this attitude that older people ain't any good anymore! We're as good as we ever were - if we ever were any good.

- Dolly Parton

The key to life is your attitude. Whether you're single or married or have kids or don't have kids, it's how you look at your life, what you make of it. It's about making the best of your life wherever you are in life.

- Candace Bushnell

When a woman puts on a heel, she has a different posture, a different attitude. She really stands up and has a consciousness of her body.

- Christian Louboutin

Eagles come in all shapes and sizes, but you will recognize them chiefly by their attitudes.

- E. F. Schumacher

Most of us start out with a positive attitude and a plan to do our best.

- Marilu Henner

When you pray for anyone you tend to modify your personal attitude toward him.

- Norman Vincent Peale

The only disability in life is a bad attitude.

- Scott Hamilton

If you get a diagnosis, get on a therapy, keep a good attitude and keep your sense of humor.

- Teri Garr

Coaches will eventually notice a great attitude, and they respect that.

- Heather O'Reilly

If you don't like something, change it. If you can't change it, change your attitude. Don't complain.

- Maya Angelou

The greatest discovery of all time is that a person can change his future by merely changing his attitude.

- Oprah Winfrey

Too much self-centered attitude, you see, brings, you see, isolation. Result: loneliness, fear, anger. The extreme self-centered attitude is the source of suffering.

- Dalai Lama

A healthy attitude is contagious but don't wait to catch it from others. Be a carrier.

- Tom Stoppard

It is very important to generate a good attitude, a good heart, as much as possible. From this, happiness in both the short term and the long term for both yourself and others will come.

- Dalai Lama

Happiness doesn't depend on any external conditions, it is governed by our mental attitude.

- Dale Carnegie

Sales are contingent upon the attitude of the salesman - not the attitude of the prospect.

- W. Clement Stone

Your attitude is like a box of crayons that color your world. Constantly color your picture gray, and your picture will always be bleak. Try adding some bright colors to the picture by including humor, and your picture begins to lighten up.

- Allen Klein

If you have a positive attitude and constantly strive to give your best effort, eventually you will overcome your immediate problems and find you are ready for greater challenges.

- Pat Riley

I will keep smiling, be positive and never give up! I will give 100 percent each time I play. These are always my goals and my attitude.

- Yani Tseng

Leadership is practiced not so much in words as in attitude and in actions.

- Harold S. Geneen

Virtually nothing is impossible in this world if you just put your mind to it and maintain a positive attitude.

- Lou Holtz

Happiness is in our own hearts. I have no regrets of anything in the past. I'm totally cheerful and happy, and I think that a lot of your attitude is not in the circumstances you find yourself in, but in the circumstances you make for yourself.

- Maeve Binchy

Always go into meetings or negotiations with a positive attitude. Tell yourself you're going to make this the best deal for all parties.

- Natalie Massenet

Like success, failure is many things to many people. With Positive Mental Attitude, failure is a learning experience, a rung on the ladder, a plateau at which to get your thoughts in order and prepare to try again.

- W. Clement Stone

It's sort of a mental attitude about critical thinking and curiosity. It's about mindset of looking at the world in a playful and curious and creative way.

- Adam Savage

Spend some time this weekend on home improvement; improve your attitude toward your family.

- Bo Bennett

I do have moments when I feel insecure. I do have moments when I feel jealous, and that's normal. It's a very normal emotion. It's your action and your attitude and your reaction to that that is important.

- Anushka Sharma

I think a lot of times we don't pay enough attention to people with a positive attitude because we assume they are naive or stupid or unschooled.

- Amy Adams

A positive attitude is something everyone can work on, and everyone can learn how to employ it.

- Joan Lunden

The winner's edge is not in a gifted birth, a high IQ, or in talent. The winner's edge is all in the attitude, not aptitude. Attitude is the criterion for success.

- Denis Waitley

You need an attitude of service. You're not just serving yourself. You help others to grow up and you grow with them.

- David Green

It's easy to get negative because you get beat down. You go through a few disappointments and it's easy to stay in that negative frame of mind. Choosing to be positive and having a grateful attitude is a whole cliché, but your attitude is going to determine how you're going to live your life.

- Joel Osteen

There's always the motivation of wanting to win. Everybody has that. But a champion needs, in his attitude, a motivation above and beyond winning.

- Pat Riley

My attitude is never to be satisfied, never enough, never.

— **Duke Ellington**

A fit body gives you confidence. And there's nothing more impressive than a great attitude, which you can wear on your sleeve. But you'll have to remember the difference between being rude and being confident.

— **Virat Kohli**

So long as you've got your friends about you, and a good positive attitude, you don't really have to care what everyone else thinks.

— **Gail Porter**

I have a very positive attitude in life. My insecurity, fear and need to know about tomorrow has fortunately eased. What is going to happen will happen anyway. So why break my head over it?

— **Katrina Kaif**

If somebody says no to you, or if you get cut, Michael Jordan was cut his first year, but he came back and he was the best ever. That is what you have to have. The attitude that I'm going to show everybody, I'm going to work hard to get better and better.

— **Magic Johnson**

Hope is a favorable and confident expectation; it's an expectant attitude that something good is going to happen and things will work out, no matter what situation we're facing.

- **Joyce Meyer**

All we need, really, is a change from a near frigid to a tropical attitude of mind.

- **Marjory Stoneman Douglas**

Commitment, belief and positive attitude are all important if you're going to be a success, whether you're in sports, in business or, as in my case, anthropology.

- **Donald Johanson**

A strong positive mental attitude will create more miracles than any wonder drug.

- **Patricia Neal**

Any fact facing us is not as important as our attitude toward it, for that determines our success or failure. The way you think about a fact may defeat you before you ever do anything about it. You are overcome by the fact because you think you are.

- **Norman Vincent Peale**

I love everybody. One of the great things about me is that I have a very positive attitude.

- **Imelda Marcos**

Whatever your situation might be, set your mind to whatever you want to do and put a good attitude in it, and I believe that you can succeed. You are not going to get anywhere just sitting on your butt and moping around.

- **Bethany Hamilton**

Success or failure in business is caused more by the mental attitude even than by mental capacities.

- **Walter Scott**

Could we change our attitude, we should not only see life differently, but life itself would come to be different.

- **Katherine Mansfield**

Regardless of the gender of the highest wage earner, the balance of power in the relationship will suffer if the higher earner uses control of the purse strings as a system of reward and punishment. It will also suffer if the lower earner takes a chippy, haughty attitude to spending money they haven't actually generated themselves.

- **Marian Keyes**

You can do everything you can to try to stop bad things from happening to you, but eventually things will happen, so the best prevention is a positive attitude.

- Marie Osmond

And the attitude of faith is the very opposite of clinging to belief, of holding on.

- Alan Watts

Your attitude towards failure determines your altitude after failure.

- John C. Maxwell

All the champions - you go and ask Mike Tyson or Joe Louis, Rocky Marciano, Lennox Lewis and myself included, and I'm sorry for putting myself in line with all the other great names - but the champion's attitude is it doesn't matter who is in front of me, I am going to conquer this person and win the fight and knock the person out.

- Wladimir Klitschko

The ABC's are attitude, behavior and communication skills.

- Gerald Chertavian

You may not be able to change a situation, but with humor you can change your attitude about it.

- Allen Klein

I have played on many teams throughout my career, and I know when a team has the tools, and the right positive attitude towards winning.

- Boomer Esiason

You can't study comedy; it's within you. It's a personality. My humor is an attitude.

- Don Rickles

Mental attitude and concentration are the keys to pitching.

- Ferguson Jenkins

Excellence is not a skill, it's an attitude.

- Ralph Marston

Being sexy is all about attitude, not body type. It's a state of mind.

- Amisha Patel

Chaotic people often have chaotic lives, and I think they create that. But if you try and have an inner peace and a positive attitude, I think you attract that.

- Imelda Staunton

Being a sex symbol has to do with an attitude, not looks. Most men think it's looks, most women know otherwise.

- Kathleen Turner

No matter what the recipe, any baker can do wonders in the kitchen with some good ingredients and an upbeat attitude!

- Buddy Valastro

When you have vision it affects your attitude. Your attitude is optimistic rather than pessimistic.

- Charles R. Swindoll

A great attitude does much more than turn on the lights in our worlds; it seems to magically connect us to all sorts of serendipitous opportunities that were somehow absent before the change.

- Earl Nightingale

Always keep that happy attitude. Pretend that you are holding a beautiful fragrant bouquet.

- Earl Nightingale

Negative attitude is nine times more powerful than positive attitude.

- Bikram Choudhury

In the business world today, failure is apparently not an option. We need to change this attitude toward failure - and celebrate the idea that only by falling on our collective business faces do we learn enough to succeed down the road.

- Naveen Jain

Prayer is talking with God. God knows your heart and is not so concerned with your words as He is with the attitude of your heart.

- Josh McDowell

If you have fun and keep a good attitude, people want to work with you.

- James Marsden

If you want small changes in your life, work on your attitude. But if you want big and primary changes, work on your paradigm.

- **Stephen Covey**

We live in a country that used to have a can-do attitude, and now we have a 'what-can-you-do-for-me?' attitude, and what I try to do is find ways that we can develop common ground.

- **Benjamin Carson**

Any of us can be happy and have a good attitude when everything is going our way. But I believe it's the real test of your character and of your faith to say, 'Things are not going our way, but I'm still being good to people; I'm still attending church; I still have a good attitude.'

- **Joel Osteen**

There was always a feeling for me that it would work. That's what keeps me going. You go in with a positive attitude and stay there, and that's a big part of what does make it work.

- **Shelley Long**

Your attitude is contagious.

- **Kevin Plank**

An attitude to life, which seeks fulfilment in the single-minded pursuit of wealth - in short, materialism - does not fit into this world, because it contains within itself no limiting principle, while the environment in which it is placed is strictly limited.

- E. F. Schumacher

I think the best advice came from Drew Barrymore, about always finding love in everything you do and keeping a positive attitude and being thankful.

- Bella Thorne

When a person doesn't have gratitude, something is missing in his or her humanity. A person can almost be defined by his or her attitude toward gratitude.

- Elie Wiesel

Today's youth are told to get rich or die trying and they really shouldn't take that attitude forward with them.

- Kareem Abdul-Jabbar

Attitude is your acceptance of the natural laws, or your rejection of the natural laws.

- Stuart Chase

It will be disastrous when a leader or manager shows up with one attitude one day and treats people with a different attitude the next day.

- Zig Ziglar

People in tough times - it doesn't mean they don't have a great attitude.

- Joel Osteen

We awaken in others the same attitude of mind we hold toward them.

- Elbert Hubbard

You tell your kids that no matter what, you set your goals and you go for them. Whatever it is you achieve, never give up. You want your kids to have that good attitude, the confidence, and the will power to believe in themselves.

- Joel Parkinson

I believe that when you think of the negative, and you get up discouraged - 'There's nothing good in my future' - I really believe it almost ties the hands of God. God works where there's an attitude of faith. I believe faith is all about hope.

- Joel Osteen

Whenever I'm having a bad day and have an attitude, I stay home. I keep it at home.

- Michael Clarke Duncan

A smart manager will establish a culture of gratitude. Expand the appreciative attitude to suppliers, vendors, delivery people, and of course, customers.

- Harvey Mackay

Choosing an attitude of faith will release peace out of your spirit and into your soul.

- Joyce Meyer

Mankind's true moral test, its fundamental test (which lies deeply buried from view), consists of its attitude towards those who are at its mercy: animals. And in this respect mankind has suffered a fundamental debacle, a debacle so fundamental that all others stem from it.

- Milan Kundera

If someone you know makes a bad decision or uses bad judgment, it doesn't mean you have to allow that to alter your attitude. Why should you allow anyone else's bad decisions to send you into a tailspin of misery?

- Joyce Meyer

I don't think it's a good attitude in your life to feel that you have to be rich to have self-esteem.

- Tom Petty

Pessimism only describes an attitude, and not facts, and hence is entirely subjective.

- Francis Parker Yockey

I think failure is nothing more than life's way of nudging you that you are off course. My attitude to failure is not attached to outcome, but in not trying. It is liberating. Most people attach failure to something not working out or how people perceive you. This way, it is about answering to yourself.

- Sara Blakely

Age and size are only numbers. It's the attitude you bring to clothes that make the difference.

- Donna Karan

Money brings you security and choice. You can make decisions in a different way if you have a lot of money. But when you have nothing, you have a naivety, and a more fearless attitude because you have nothing to lose.

- Simon Cowell

To make flexibility work, it is not only necessary to change our attitude about who is a good worker and who is not, but we have to train managers at all levels to recognize the difference between the number of hours worked and the quality of work produced.

- **Madeleine M. Kunin**

It's a question of keeping one's eyes and ears open and watching how other people play the game. They're watching me too, to see what my attitude is like.

- **Charles Dance**

If you can't change your fate, change your attitude.

- **Charles Revson**

If you have an ongoing relationship with a person, think of everything positive about that person that you possibly can and enter your interaction from that space. Ignore all the crap that used to drive you up the wall before. You will be amazed at what a change this attitude shift brings about.

- **Srikumar Rao**

You don't have to have an attitude if you're famous.

- **Adriana Lima**

Seek out that particular mental attribute which makes you feel most deeply and vitally alive, along with which comes the inner voice which says, 'This is the real me,' and when you have found that attitude, follow it.

- James Truslow Adams

The time I spent thinking about how I was better than somebody else or worrying about somebody else's attitude was time I could put to better use.

- Charley Pride

All ideas come about through some sort of observation. It sparks an attitude; some object or emotion causes a reaction in the other person.

- Graham Chapman

Only one thing can conquer war - that attitude of mind which can see nothing in war but destruction and annihilation.

- Ludwig von Mises

I was bringing my attitude as a regular person 'cause this is my attitude'.

- Glenn Danzig

My deepest impulses are optimistic, an attitude that seems to me as spiritually necessary and proper as it is intellectually suspect.

- **Ellen Willis**

Life is about challenges and how we face up to them and the attitude we take into every day life so hopefully we'll be able to motivate people to do more with their life.

- **Martina Navratilova**

Even if people do wrong, we're social animals, so what can we do about stopping them doing the same things in future? Saying people are 'bad' or 'evil' is just an unwillingness to engage; an unwillingness to try to empathise. That sanctimonious attitude doesn't help anyone.

- **Denise Mina**

We have the ability to craft a life where we are completely fulfilled. We think it is dependent on outsiders, and to some extent it is, but it is much more dependent on the attitude we bring to life.

- **Srikumar Rao**

I walk tall; I got a tall attitude.

- **Dolly Parton**

You can't be a crazy rebel in the face of death; it's not a fitting attitude.

- **Michel Houellebecq**

A black suit can be classic and timeless and certainly for most occasions. But remember, it's not so much the color of suit as it is about the fit, cut, style, and, of course, attitude you have when wearing it.

- **John Varvatos**

If a person can be said to have the wrong attitude, there is no need to pay attention to his arguments.

- **John McCarthy**

You can learn what you want to learn through hard work. And a good employer will teach you what you want to learn as long as you show the right attitude and behaviors.

- **Gerald Chertavian**

Maybe its just parenthood that puts you in a situation where you just have to develop a new attitude, I guess, about things.

- **James Mercer**

Each experience through which we pass operates ultimately for our good. This is a correct attitude to adopt and we must be able to see it in that light.

- Henry S. Haskins

If wearing the Spanx helps you get looks, and you feel that energy and response, and you're rocking your body with confidence, that's still how you'll feel about yourself when you get home and take the Spanx off... If your attitude improves from the Spanx, wear the Spanx!

- Lisa Ann Walter

Let us change our traditional attitude to the construction of programs. Instead of imagining that our main task is to instruct a computer what to do, let us concentrate rather on explaining to human beings what we want a computer to do.

- Donald Knuth

When you are facing the wilderness on your own, you have a totally different attitude to someone who works in government or who has a monthly cheque.

- Rick Santelli

Refuse to be a lazy Christian, and resist a passive, apathetic attitude.

- Joyce Meyer

I think it's important and I think it's true that our life experience is going to be about our attitude, our thoughts, our beliefs, our speech and our actions. We can transform our life experience simply by changing our language.

- **Jason Mraz**

I didn't know how to show my self-love, and I didn't want anyone else to hurt me. So my tough girl attitude was like, 'I'm not having it.'

- **Mary J. Blige**

I've never run into a guy who could win at the top level in anything today and didn't have the right attitude, didn't give it everything he had, at least while he was doing it; wasn't prepared and didn't have the whole program worked out.

- **Ted Turner**

My attitude is, do as much as I can while I'm free. And if I'm arrested I'll still do as much as I can.

- **Aung San Suu Kyi**

The characteristic political attitude of today is not one of positive belief, but of despair.

- **Herbert Read**

One day I looked in the mirror, and I wasn't happy. If you're not feeling good mentally, emotionally and physically, you're just a mess - and that's the point I felt like. It was a change in attitude and a shift in lifestyle. There's no crazy diet; I train six days a week, and I eat really well.

- Ricki-Lee Coulter

You have to have an attitude that nothing's gonna stop me. I think that's just my New York kind of attitude - survival of the fittest.

- Melissa De Sousa

My father instilled in me the attitude of prevailing. If there's a challenge, go for it. If there's a wall to break down, break it down.

- Donny Osmond

When you retire, it's a place in life, a part of the journey. You just don't quit work; you develop an attitude where you can do what you please.

- Tom T. Hall

A discipline I have observed is an attitude of love and reverence to people.

- Bessie Head

If you can attribute your success entirely to your own mental effort, to your own attitude, to some spiritual essence that you have that is better than other people's, then that must feel pretty good.

- Barbara Ehrenreich

There is an attitude that we should be able to have everything. No, you shouldn't be able to have anything. I'd like a helicopter, but I can't afford a helicopter, so I don't buy one. People are buying stuff they can't afford on credit. I bought my Ford hybrid with cash.

- Grace Slick

We have all met people that act 'old' or think a number makes them old, and I truly don't believe that is the case. If you have a good attitude toward aging, and you do what you can to live healthy and take care of yourself, I don't think the number matters.

- Tabatha Coffey

I was always spiritual, even as a child. I was taught to pray, show gratitude. We had an attitude of gratitude. Even if life was ugly, bad or sad - we prayed.

- Shilpa Shetty

I think the truth is, we are all racist, really, when it comes down to it. I think all of us have to check ourselves from time to time, and say, 'Look, that sort of attitude isn't good enough.' It takes discipline to keep our prejudices out.

- Peter Hollingworth

Our spiritual attitude is determined by our conception of our relation to infinite spirit.

- Paul Twitchell

I've never been in any country for more than four years, and I'm learning different languages all the time. It gives you a different attitude.

- Santiago Cabrera

I have the same attitude with work - I like to go to work, I like to work really hard I, like to give everything my all, I like to try things that are new, you know.

- Rosie Huntington-Whiteley

Design is about point of view, and there should be some sort of woman or lifestyle or attitude in one's head as a designer. So my being able to reach the masses was something that meant a great deal to me - especially for women who could never wear Vera Wang.

- Vera Wang

You lose attitude when you feel too comfortable, so I prefer to wear clothes that have a certain edge to them.

- Carine Roitfeld

I certainly don't disparage someone whose attitude towards their work is utterly different from mine - that's up to them.

- Ian Mckellen

I love a woman with a relaxed attitude.

- Stephane Rolland

I have met so many people who are negative, and it tells on their attitude towards life and towards everything.

- Phaneesh Murthy

Britishness is just a way of putting things together and a certain don't care attitude about clothes. You don't care, you just do it and it looks great.

- Vivienne Westwood

As a life coach, I love makeovers, from new clothes to surgery, pedicures to highlights. But redoing makes you feel better only if approached with the right attitude.

- Martha Beck

I can pull off anything; I have the height and the attitude. The only thing I can't wear is a leotard, but I can wear anything else.

- **Theophilus London**

The most important criterion is this: hire someone whose character and humility and attitude you would like to have reproduced in your church and in yourself.

- **John Ortberg**

Children have adopted a consumerist attitude - I dare you to entertain me.

- **Walter Dean Myers**

I have such an extreme attitude about work, where I can just completely be derelict of my responsibilities and then when I am not derelict, I am completely indulged in it. I swing pretty wildly from the two extremes.

- **Geddy Lee**

Part of our western outlook stems from the scientific attitude and its method of isolating the parts of a phenomenon in order to analyze them.

- **Arthur Erickson**

I think it has something to do with being British. We don't take ourselves as seriously as some other countries do. I think a lot of people take themselves far too seriously; I find that a very tedious attitude.

- **Joan Collins**

If you eat something and get fat, you should be responsible for it. I think that is the attitude of the great majority of Americans that you should be responsible for what you eat.

- **Vic Snyder**

I kind of resent this attitude of men that we somehow must always look good.

- **Sharon Gless**

You can have a laugh in Los Angeles, or you can weep in Los Angeles, depending on your attitude towards it.

- **Miranda Richardson**

It really was hand-to-mouth and you can say, 'Poor little me, how dreadful, what a deprived childhood', but I didn't feel that way at all. It's all about the attitude at home.

- **Carol Vorderman**

Fame is O.K. I hate it, but it's O.K. I'm beginning to understand how I can be hidden. It's an attitude.

- Romain Duris

Part of the whole L.A. mentality that nothing really matters unless it's a success... is such a shallow and dangerous attitude to have.

- Patricia Richardson

The American attitude towards efficiency and execution should always underlie architecture.

- Helmut Jahn

<u>Wisdom</u>

The only true wisdom is in knowing you know nothing.

- Socrates

He who lives in harmony with himself lives in harmony with the universe.

- Marcus Aurelius

Do not go where the path may lead, go instead where there is no path and leave a trail.

- Ralph Waldo Emerson

A man must be big enough to admit his mistakes, smart enough to profit from them, and strong enough to correct them.

- John C. Maxwell

We cannot become what we need to be by remaining what we are.

- Max de Pree

A day of worry is more exhausting than a week of work.

- John Lubbock

The pessimist complains about the wind; the optimist expects it to change; the realist adjusts the sails.

- William Arthur Ward

Everything that irritates us about others can lead us to an understanding of ourselves.

- Carl Jung

Talent is God given. Be humble. Fame is man-given. Be grateful. Conceit is self-given. Be careful.

- John Wooden

Beware of false knowledge; it is more dangerous than ignorance.

- George Bernard Shaw

The higher we are placed, the more humbly we should walk.

- Marcus Tullius Cicero

It's not what you look at that matters, it's what you see.

- Henry David Thoreau

Discipline is the bridge between goals and accomplishment.

- Jim Rohn

A long habit of not thinking a thing wrong gives it a superficial appearance of being right.

- Thomas Paine

Never interrupt someone doing what you said couldn't be done.

- Amelia Earhart

The journey of a thousand miles begins with one step.

- Lao Tzu

The more you like yourself, the less you are like anyone else, which makes you unique.

- Walt Disney

If you're trying to achieve, there will be roadblocks. I've had them; everybody has had them. But obstacles don't have to stop you. If you run into a wall, don't turn around and give up. Figure out how to climb it, go through it, or work around it.

- Michael Jordan

For beautiful eyes, look for the good in others; for beautiful lips, speak only words of kindness; and for poise, walk with the knowledge that you are never alone.

- Audrey Hepburn

A good head and a good heart are always a formidable combination.

- Nelson Mandela

When it is obvious that the goals cannot be reached, don't adjust the goals, adjust the action steps.

- Confucius

We are what our thoughts have made us; so take care about what you think. Words are secondary. Thoughts live; they travel far.

- Swami Vivekananda

People spend too much time finding other people to blame, too much energy finding excuses for not being what they are capable of being, and not enough energy putting themselves on the line, growing out of the past, and getting on with their lives.

- J. Michael Straczynski

The best way to destroy an enemy is to make him a friend.
- Abraham Lincoln

Be happy. It's one way of being wise.
- Sidonie Gabrielle Colette

Wisdom begins in wonder.
- Socrates

From the errors of others, a wise man corrects his own.
- Publilius Syrus

Being entirely honest with oneself is a good exercise.
- Sigmund Freud

We are made wise not by the recollection of our past, but by the responsibility for our future.
- George Bernard Shaw

It is a common experience that a problem difficult at night is resolved in the morning after the committee of sleep has worked on it.
- John Steinbeck

I have just three things to teach: simplicity, patience, compassion. These three are your greatest treasures.

- Lao Tzu

Whatever you do in life, surround yourself with smart people who'll argue with you.

- John Wooden

Experience is not what happens to you; it's what you do with what happens to you.

- Aldous Huxley

My father said there were two kinds of people in the world: givers and takers. The takers may eat better, but the givers sleep better.

- Marlo Thomas

A tree is known by its fruit; a man by his deeds. A good deed is never lost; he who sows courtesy reaps friendship, and he who plants kindness gathers love.

- Saint Basil

Reality is merely an illusion, albeit a very persistent one.

- Albert Einstein

One's philosophy is not best expressed in words; it is expressed in the choices one makes... and the choices we make are ultimately our responsibility.

- Eleanor Roosevelt

Start with what is right rather than what is acceptable.

- Franz Kafka

Never let your head hang down. Never give up and sit down and grieve. Find another way. And don't pray when it rains if you don't pray when the sun shines.

- Richard M. Nixon

The greater danger for most of us lies not in setting our aim too high and falling short; but in setting our aim too low, and achieving our mark.

- Michelangelo

Everything comes to us that belongs to us if we create the capacity to receive it.

- Rabindranath Tagore

You've got to go out on a limb sometimes because that's where the fruit is.

- Will Rogers

True wisdom comes to each of us when we realize how little we understand about life, ourselves, and the world around us.

- Socrates

If you talk to a man in a language he understands, that goes to his head. If you talk to him in his language, that goes to his heart.

- Nelson Mandela

People don't notice whether it's winter or summer when they're happy.

- Anton Chekhov

In dwelling, live close to the ground. In thinking, keep to the simple. In conflict, be fair and generous. In governing, don't try to control. In work, do what you enjoy. In family life, be completely present.

- Lao Tzu

Always be a first-rate version of yourself, instead of a second-rate version of somebody else.

- Judy Garland

Honesty is the best policy.

- Benjamin Franklin

With pride, there are many curses. With humility, there come many blessings.

- Ezra Taft Benson

If you don't know where you are going, any road will get you there.

- Lewis Carroll

It requires wisdom to understand wisdom: the music is nothing if the audience is deaf.

- Walter Lippmann

The way you see people is the way you treat them, and the way you treat them is what they become.

- Johann Wolfgang von Goethe

Never tell people how to do things. Tell them what to do and they will surprise you with their ingenuity.

- George S. Patton

Obstacles are those frightful things you see when you take your eyes off your goal.

- Henry Ford

Wisdom, compassion, and courage are the three universally recognized moral qualities of men.

- Confucius

Knowing others is wisdom, knowing yourself is Enlightenment.

- Lao Tzu

Always seek out the seed of triumph in every adversity.

- Og Mandino

It has long been an axiom of mine that the little things are infinitely the most important.

- Arthur Conan Doyle

Give me a lever long enough and a fulcrum on which to place it, and I shall move the world.

- Archimedes

Yesterday is history, tomorrow is a mystery, today is God's gift, that's why we call it the present.

- Joan Rivers

Plodding wins the race.

- Aesop

Even if you're on the right track, you'll get run over if you just sit there.

- Will Rogers

It's better to be a lion for a day than a sheep all your life.

- Elizabeth Kenny

Winning is not everything, but wanting to win is.

- Vince Lombardi

When you give yourself, you receive more than you give.

- Antoine de Saint-Exupery

A fool flatters himself, a wise man flatters the fool.

- Edward G. Bulwer-Lytton

It is the nature of the wise to resist pleasures, but the foolish to be a slave to them.

- Epictetus

Set your course by the stars, not by the lights of every passing ship.

- Omar N. Bradley

That old law about 'an eye for an eye' leaves everybody blind. The time is always right to do the right thing.

- Martin Luther King, Jr.

A wise man is superior to any insults which can be put upon him, and the best reply to unseemly behavior is patience and moderation.

- Moliere

Spectacular achievement is always preceded by unspectacular preparation.

- Robert H. Schuller

If you only have a hammer, you tend to see every problem as a nail.

- Abraham Maslow

Always keep an open mind and a compassionate heart.

- Phil Jackson

The golden opportunity you are seeking is in yourself. It is not in your environment; it is not in luck or chance, or the help of others; it is in yourself alone.

- Orison Swett Marden

Knowledge is proud that it knows so much; wisdom is humble that it knows no more.

- William Cowper

Wise sayings often fall on barren ground, but a kind word is never thrown away.

- Arthur Helps

Turn your wounds into wisdom.

- Oprah Winfrey

The best way to obtain truth and wisdom is not to ask from books, but to go to God in prayer, and obtain divine teaching.

- Joseph Smith, Jr.

Talent is God-given; be humble. Fame is man-given; be thankful. Conceit is self-given; be careful.

- Harvey Mackay

Giving opens the way for receiving.

- Florence Scovel Shinn

The greatest obstacle to discovery is not ignorance - it is the illusion of knowledge.

- Daniel J. Boorstin

This is what I learned: that everybody is talented, original and has something important to say.

- Brenda Ueland

To be satisfied with a little, is the greatest wisdom; and he that increaseth his riches, increaseth his cares; but a contented mind is a hidden treasure, and trouble findeth it not.

- Akhenaton

Quick decisions are unsafe decisions.

- Sophocles

When written in Chinese, the word 'crisis' is composed of two characters. One represents danger and the other represents opportunity.

- John F. Kennedy

Start wide, expand further, and never look back.

- Arnold Schwarzenegger

Appearances are often deceiving.

- Aesop

The young man knows the rules, but the old man knows the exceptions.

- Oliver Wendell Holmes, Sr.

Ignorant men raise questions that wise men answered a thousand years ago.

- Johann Wolfgang von Goethe

The truth is not for all men, but only for those who seek it.

- Ayn Rand

The time to repair the roof is when the sun is shining.

- John F. Kennedy

The opportunity for brotherhood presents itself every time you meet a human being.

- **Jane Wyman**

If you do not express your own original ideas, if you do not listen to your own being, you will have betrayed yourself.

- **Rollo May**

It is better to risk starving to death then surrender. If you give up on your dreams, what's left?

- **Jim Carrey**

You can't sweep other people off their feet, if you can't be swept off your own.

- **Clarence Day**

The lure of the distant and the difficult is deceptive. The great opportunity is where you are.

- **John Burroughs**

Wisdom ceases to be wisdom when it becomes too proud to weep, too grave to laugh, and too selfish to seek other than itself.

- **Khalil Gibran**

Never reach out your hand unless you're willing to extend an arm.

- **Pope Paul VI**

To wear your heart on your sleeve isn't a very good plan; you should wear it inside, where it functions best.

- **Margaret Thatcher**

Dost thou love life? Then do not squander time, for that is the stuff life is made of.

- **Benjamin Franklin**

Perhaps too much of everything is as bad as too little.

- **Edna Ferber**

You must accept responsibility for your actions, but not the credit for your achievements.

- **Denis Waitley**

We should not judge people by their peak of excellence; but by the distance they have travelled from the point where they started.

- **Henry Ward Beecher**

Adopt the pace of nature: her secret is patience.

- Ralph Waldo Emerson

Don't taunt the alligator until after you've crossed the creek.

- Dan Rather

The greater our knowledge increases the more our ignorance unfolds.

- John F. Kennedy

Nothing that you have not given away will ever be really yours.

- C. S. Lewis

Wise men make more opportunities than they find.

- Francis Bacon

Patience is the companion of wisdom.

- Saint Augustine

The motto of chivalry is also the motto of wisdom; to serve all, but love only one.

- Honore de Balzac

The art of being wise is the art of knowing what to overlook.

- William James

The man of knowledge must be able not only to love his enemies but also to hate his friends.

- Friedrich Nietzsche

The smallest deed is better than the greatest intention.

- John Burroughs

Wisdom is the reward you get for a lifetime of listening when you'd have preferred to talk.

- Doug Larson

Regret for the things we did can be tempered by time; it is regret for the things we did not do that is inconsolable.

- Sydney J. Harris

Only put off until tomorrow what you are willing to die having left undone.

- Pablo Picasso

A man begins cutting his wisdom teeth the first time he bites off more than he can chew.

- Herb Caen

It is like the seed put in the soil - the more one sows, the greater the harvest.

- Orison Swett Marden

This is the highest wisdom that I own; freedom and life are earned by those alone who conquer them each day anew.

- Johann Wolfgang von Goethe

The chief condition on which, life, health and vigor depend on, is action. It is by action that an organism develops its faculties, increases its energy, and attains the fulfilment of its destiny.

- Colin Powell

Wisdom stands at the turn in the road and calls upon us publicly, but we consider it false and despise its adherents.

- Khalil Gibran

Cleverness is not wisdom.

- Euripides

Habit is the nursery of errors.

- Victor Hugo

If you want to go east, don't go west.

- Ramakrishna

The doorstep to the temple of wisdom is a knowledge of our own ignorance.

- Benjamin Franklin

Self-suggestion makes you master of yourself.

- W. Clement Stone

Imagination is more important than knowledge.

- Sylvia Plath

The wheel that squeaks the loudest is the one that gets the grease.

- Josh Billings

Fear cannot be without hope nor hope without fear.

- Baruch Spinoza

Wisdom is the power to put our time and our knowledge to the proper use.

- Thomas J. Watson

Don't follow any advice, no matter how good, until you feel as deeply in your spirit as you think in your mind that the counsel is wise.

- Joan Rivers

Wisdom is not wisdom when it is derived from books alone.

- Horace

A heart well prepared for adversity in bad times hopes, and in good times fears for a change in fortune.

- Horace

Deliberately seek opportunities for kindness, sympathy, and patience.

- Evelyn Underhill

Public opinion is no more than this: what people think that other people think.

- Alfred Austin

There is a wisdom of the head, and a wisdom of the heart.

- Charles Dickens

The superior man blames himself. The inferior man blames others.

- Don Shula

You can't cross the sea merely by standing and staring at the water. Don't let yourself indulge in vain wishes.

- Laurence J. Peter

Make it your habit not to be critical about small things.

- Edward Everett Hale

Each of us has been put on earth with the ability to do something well. We cheat ourselves and the world if we don't use that ability as best we can.

- George Allen, Sr.

The sweetest of all sounds is praise.

- Xenophon

No man was ever wise by chance.

- Lucius Annaeus Seneca

The more one pleases everybody, the less one pleases profoundly.

- Stendhal

Memory is the mother of all wisdom.

- Aeschylus

Man's wisdom is his best friend; folly his worst enemy.

- William Temple

Learning sleeps and snores in libraries, but wisdom is everywhere, wide-awake, on tiptoe.

- Josh Billings

Wisdom is knowing what to do next; virtue is doing it.

- David Starr Jordan

The best way to predict the future is to invent it.

- Alan Kay

It takes a great man to give sound advice tactfully, but a greater man to accept it graciously.

- Logan Pearsall Smith

All of us, at certain moments of our lives, need to take advice and to receive help from other people.

- Alexis Carrel

Nature and books belong to the eyes that see them.

- Ralph Waldo Emerson

If I don't have wisdom, I can teach you only ignorance.

- Leo Buscaglia

The older I grow the more I distrust the familiar doctrine that age brings wisdom.

- H. L. Mencken

It is while you are patiently toiling at the little tasks of life that the meaning and shape of the great whole of life dawn on you.

- Phillips Brooks

When an opponent comes forward, move in and greet him; if he wants to pull back, send him on his way.

- Morihei Ueshiba

A mouse does not rely on just one hole.

- Plautus

Look twice before you leap.

- Charlotte Bronte

All this worldly wisdom was once the unamiable heresy of some wise man.

- Henry David Thoreau

Repeat anything often enough and it will start to become you.

- Tom Hopkins

A mistake is simply another way of doing things.

- Katharine Graham

Wisdom doesn't necessarily come with age. Sometimes age just shows up all by itself.

- Tom Wilson

Common sense in an uncommon degree is what the world calls wisdom.

- Samuel Taylor Coleridge

A little knowledge that acts is worth infinitely more than much knowledge that is idle.

- Khalil Gibran

Good nature is worth more than knowledge, more than money, more than honor, to the persons who possess it.

- Henry Ward Beecher

The less you talk, the more you're listened to.

- Pauline Phillips

To conquer fear is the beginning of wisdom.

- Bertrand Russell

The more sand that has escaped from the hourglass of our life, the clearer we should see through it.

- Jean Paul

Please all, and you will please none.

- Aesop

It is the neglect of timely repair that makes rebuilding necessary.

- Richard Whately

Wisdom is always an overmatch for strength.

- Phil Jackson

It is a characteristic of wisdom not to do desperate things.

- Henry David Thoreau

Wisdom is found only in truth.

- Johann Wolfgang von Goethe

A prudent question is one-half of wisdom.

- Francis Bacon

It's not the having, it's the getting.

- Elizabeth Taylor

Rarely promise, but, if lawful, constantly perform.

- William Penn

Suffering is one of life's great teachers.

- Bryant H. McGill

We are wiser than we know.

- Ralph Waldo Emerson

If you wish to reach the highest, begin at the lowest.

- Publilius Syrus

The wisdom of the wise and the experience of the ages are perpetuated by quotations.

- Benjamin Disraeli

If you want to be found stand where the seeker seeks.

- Sidney Lanier

Wisdom outweighs any wealth.

- Sophocles

Few of the many wise apothegms which have been uttered have prevented a single foolish action.

- Thomas Babington Macaulay

Strong characters are brought out by change of situation, and gentle ones by permanence.

- Jean Paul

It is the mind that maketh good or ill, that maketh wretch or happy, rich or poor.

- Michel de Montaigne

I didn't get where I am today by worryin' about how I'd feel tomorrow.

- Ron White

Man is only great when he acts from passion.

- Benjamin Disraeli

Never cut what you can untie.

- Joseph Joubert

Almost every wise saying has an opposite one, no less wise, to balance it.

- George Santayana

When you doubt, abstain.

- Ambrose Bierce

The fall of dropping water wears away the stone.

- Lucretius

Wisdom is the quality that keeps you from getting into situations where you need it.

- Doug Larson

Let deeds match words.

- Plautus

Perspective is worth 80 IQ points.

- Alan Kay

Above all, you must fight conceit, envy, and every kind of ill-feeling in your heart.

- Abraham Cahan

He who devotes sixteen hours a day to hard study may become at sixty as wise as he thought himself at twenty.

- Mary Wilson Little

The wisdom of the wise is an uncommon degree of common sense.

- Dean Inge

All human wisdom works and has worries and grief as reward.

- Johann Georg Hamann

When defeat is inevitable, it is wisest to yield.

- Quintilian

Counsel woven into the fabric of real life is wisdom.

- Walter Benjamin

It is much more difficult to measure non-performance than performance.

- Harold S. Geneen

What is man's ultimate direction in life? It is to look for love, truth, virtue, and beauty.

- Shinichi Suzuki

Never does nature say one thing and wisdom another.

- Juvenal

Some folks are wise and some are otherwise.

- Tobias Smollett

When I can look life in the eyes, grown calm and very coldly wise, life will have given me the truth, and taken in exchange - my youth.

- Sara Teasdale

Of prosperity mortals can never have enough.

- Aeschylus

To advise is not to compel.

- Anton Chekhov

Wisdom begins at the end.

- Daniel Webster

Wisdom we know is the knowledge of good and evil, not the strength to choose between the two.

- John Cheever

In seeking wisdom thou art wise; in imagining that thou hast attained it - thou art a fool.

- Philip Stanhope, 4th Earl of Chesterfield

Logic is the beginning of wisdom, not the end.

- Leonard Nimoy

Music is a higher revelation than all wisdom and philosophy.

- Ludwig van Beethoven

To enjoy good health, to bring true happiness to one's family, to bring peace to all, one must first discipline and control one's own mind. If a man can control his mind he can find the way to Enlightenment, and all wisdom and virtue will naturally come to him.

- Buddha

The man who makes everything that leads to happiness depends upon himself, and not upon other men, has adopted the very best plan for living happily. This is the man of moderation, the man of manly character and of wisdom.

- Plato

Where there is charity and wisdom, there is neither fear nor ignorance.

- Francis of Assisi

Those who improve with age embrace the power of personal growth and personal achievement and begin to replace youth with wisdom, innocence with understanding, and lack of purpose with self-actualization.

- Bo Bennett

God grant me the serenity to accept the things I cannot change, the courage to change the things I can, and the wisdom to know the difference.

- Reinhold Niebuhr

Honesty is the first chapter in the book of wisdom.

- Thomas Jefferson

Don't gain the world and lose your soul; wisdom is better than silver or gold.

- Bob Marley

Wisdom is the right use of knowledge. To know is not to be wise. Many men know a great deal, and are all the greater fools for it. There is no fool so great a fool as a knowing fool. But to know how to use knowledge is to have wisdom.

- Charles Spurgeon

Science is organized knowledge. Wisdom is organized life.

- Immanuel Kant

To acquire knowledge, one must study; but to acquire wisdom, one must observe.

- Marilyn vos Savant

Knowledge speaks, but wisdom listens.

- Jimi Hendrix

To make no mistakes is not in the power of man; but from their errors and mistakes the wise and good learn wisdom for the future.

- Plutarch

By the time you've reached your sixties, you do know that one-day you will die, and knowing that is at least the beginning of wisdom.

- Terry Pratchett

The philosophy of life is this: Life is not a struggle, not a tension... Life is bliss. It is eternal wisdom, eternal existence.

- Maharishi Mahesh Yogi

The saddest aspect of life right now is that science gathers knowledge faster than society gathers wisdom.

- Isaac Asimov

Logic is the beginning of wisdom, not the end.

- Leonard Nimoy

It is not wisdom but Authority that makes a law.

- **Thomas Hobbes**

There is a difference between happiness and wisdom: he that thinks himself the happiest man is really so; but he that thinks himself the wisest is generally the greatest fool.

- **Francis Bacon**

We must expect reverses, even defeats. They are sent to teach us wisdom and prudence, to call forth greater energies, and to prevent our falling into greater disasters.

- **Robert E. Lee**

Knowledge is knowing that a tomato is a fruit. Wisdom is knowing not to put it in a fruit salad.

- **Brian O'Driscoll**

If you are bitter, you are like a dry leaf that you can just squash, and you can get blown away by the wind. There is much more wisdom in forgiveness.

- **Vusi Mahlasela**

The attempt to combine wisdom and power has only rarely been successful and then only for a short while.

- **Albert Einstein**

In youth and beauty, wisdom is but rare!

- Homer

Kindness is more important than wisdom, and the recognition of this is the beginning of wisdom.

- Theodore Isaac Rubin

Vanity can easily overtake wisdom. It usually overtakes common sense.

- Julian Casablancas

Strength and wisdom are not opposing values.

- William J. Clinton

Data is not information, information is not knowledge, knowledge is not understanding, understanding is not wisdom.

- Clifford Stoll

We humans have lost the wisdom of genuinely resting and relaxing. We worry too much. We don't allow our bodies to heal, and we don't allow our minds and hearts to heal.

- Thich Nhat Hanh

We don't receive wisdom; we must discover it for ourselves after a journey that no one can take for us or spare us.

- Marcel Proust

If we continue to develop our technology without wisdom or prudence, our servant may prove to be our executioner.

- Omar N. Bradley

True wisdom is less presuming than folly. The wise man doubteth often, and changeth his mind; the fool is obstinate, and doubteth not; he knoweth all things but his own ignorance.

- Akhenaton

In life, all good things come hard, but wisdom is the hardest to come by.

- Lucille Ball

Irony is the gaiety of reflection and the joy of wisdom.

- Anatole France

They must often change, who would be constant in happiness or wisdom.

- Confucius

Every day, every birthday candle I blow out, every penny I throw over my shoulder in a wishing well, every time my daughter says, 'Let's make a wish on a star,' there's one thing I wish for: wisdom.

- Rene Russo

Start with God - the first step in learning is bowing down to God; only fools thumb their noses at such wisdom and learning.

- King Solomon

Silence is true wisdom's best reply.

- Euripides

It is unwise to be too sure of one's own wisdom. It is healthy to be reminded that the strongest might weaken and the wisest might err.

- Mahatma Gandhi

I hope our wisdom will grow with our power, and teach us, that the less we use our power the greater it will be.

- Thomas Jefferson

Great wisdom is generous; petty wisdom is contentious.

- Zhuangzi

If I am a fool, it is, at least, a doubting one; and I envy no one the certainty of his self-approved wisdom.

- Lord Byron

With age comes common sense and wisdom.

- Nas

Mistakes are the usual bridge between inexperience and wisdom.

- Phyllis Theroux

Wisdom and understanding can only become the possession of individual men by travelling the old road of observation, attention, perseverance, and industry.

- Samuel Smiles

Doubt is the vestibule through which all must pass before they can enter into the temple of wisdom.

- Charles Caleb Colton

Books are the ever-burning lamps of accumulated wisdom.

- George William Curtis

We learn wisdom from failure much more than from success. We often discover what will do, by finding out what will not do; and probably he who never made a mistake never made a discovery.

- Samuel Smiles

In complete darkness we are all the same, it is only our knowledge and wisdom that separates us, don't let your eyes deceive you.

- Janet Jackson

There is more wisdom in your body than in your deepest philosophy.

- Friedrich Nietzsche

The key to wisdom is this - constant and frequent questioning, for by doubting we are led to question and by questioning we arrive at the truth.

- Peter Abelard

The more tranquil a man becomes, the greater is his success, his influence, his power for good. Calmness of mind is one of the beautiful jewels of wisdom.

- James Allen

Follow your instincts. That's where true wisdom manifests itself.

- Oprah Winfrey

The pine stays green in winter... wisdom in hardship.

- Norman Douglas

If you have the guts to keep making mistakes, your wisdom and intelligence leap forward with huge momentum.

- Holly Near

The gateways to wisdom and learning are always open, and more and more I am choosing to walk through them. Barriers, blocks, obstacles, and problems are personal teachers giving me the opportunity to move out of the past and into the Totality of Possibilities.

- Louise L. Hay

History is filled with tragic examples of wars that result from diplomatic impasse. Whether in our local communities or in international relations, the skilful use of our communicative capacities to negotiate and resolve differences, is the first evidence of human wisdom.

- Daisaku Ikeda

When we looked at the life cycle in our 40s, we looked to old people for wisdom. At 80, though, we look at other 80-year-olds to see who got wise and who not. Lots of old people don't get wise, but you don't get wise unless you age.

- **Erik Erikson**

Sometimes I am happy and sometimes not. I am, after all, a human being, you know. And I am glad that we are sometimes happy and sometimes not. You get your wisdom working by having different emotions.

- **Yoko Ono**

The wisdom of the wise, and the experience of ages, may be preserved by quotation.

- **Isaac D'Israeli**

Pain and foolishness lead to great bliss and complete knowledge, for Eternal Wisdom created nothing under the sun in vain.

- **Khalil Gibran**

Many sophisticated, intelligent people lack wisdom and common sense.

- **Joyce Meyer**

Wisdom is oftentimes nearer when we stoop than when we soar.

- William Wordsworth

Through consciousness, our minds have the power to change our planet and ourselves. It is time we heed the wisdom of the ancient indigenous people and channel our consciousness and spirit to tend the garden and not destroy it.

- Bruce Lipton

A man may learn wisdom even from a foe.

- Aristophanes

Few people have the wisdom to prefer the criticism that would do them good, to the praise that deceives them.

- Francois de La Rochefoucauld

We can be knowledgeable with other men's knowledge but we cannot be wise with other men's wisdom.

- Michel de Montaigne

There's a beauty to wisdom and experience that cannot be faked. It's impossible to be mature without having lived.

- Amy Grant

Preconceived notions are the locks on the door to wisdom.

- **Mary Browne**

It is astonishing what force, purity, and wisdom it requires for a human being to keep clear of falsehoods.

- **Margaret Fuller**

Imagination allows us to escape the predictable. It enables us to reply to the common wisdom that we cannot soar by saying, 'Just watch!'

- **Bill Bradley**

I have studied many philosophers and many cats. The wisdom of cats is infinitely superior.

- **Hippolyte Taine**

This age thinks better of a gilded fool than of a threadbare saint in wisdom's school.

- **Thomas Dekker**

Whenever you argue with another wiser than yourself in order that others may admire your wisdom, they will discover your ignorance.

- **Saadi**

Science gives us knowledge, but only philosophy can give us wisdom.

- **Will Durant**

Not engaging in ignorance is wisdom.

- **Bodhidharma**

The function of wisdom is to discriminate between good and evil.

- **Marcus Tullius Cicero**

If we have built on the fragile cornerstones of human wisdom, pride, and conditional love, things may look good for a while, but a weak foundation causes collapse when storms hit.

- **Charles Stanley**

The greatest wisdom is to realize one's lack of it.

- **Constantin Stanislavski**

Wisdom does not show itself so much in precept as in life - in firmness of mind and a mastery of appetite. It teaches us to do as well as to talk; and to make our words and actions all of a color.

- **Lucius Annaeus Seneca**

Back of every mistaken venture and defeat is the laughter of wisdom, if you listen.

- **Carl Sandburg**

Discipline is wisdom and vice versa.

- **M. Scott Peck**

Lord, bless me with the ability to achieve all that I can, and the wisdom to realize it doesn't all have to be by tomorrow!

- **William Eardley IV**

As you walk in God's divine wisdom, you will surely begin to see a greater measure of victory and good success in your life.

- **Joseph Prince**

Pain makes man think. Thought makes man wise. Wisdom makes life endurable.

- **John Patrick**

More helpful than all wisdom is one draught of simple human pity that will not forsake us.

- **George Eliot**

If you have the insight of non-self, if you have the insight of impermanence, you should make that insight into a concentration that you keep alive throughout the day. Then what you say, what you think, and what you do will then be in the light of that wisdom and you will avoid making mistakes and creating suffering.

- Thich Nhat Hanh

I'm not wise, but the beginning of wisdom is there; it's like relaxing into - and an acceptance of - things.

- Tina Turner

The wisdom of the wise and the experience of the ages is preserved into perpetuity by a nation's proverbs, fables, folk sayings and quotations.

- William Feather

More helpful than all wisdom is one draught of simple human pity that will not forsake us.

- George Eliot

Most of our pocket wisdom is conceived for the use of mediocre people, to discourage them from ambitious attempts, and generally console them in their mediocrity.

- Robert Louis Stevenson

Before we acquire great power we must acquire wisdom to use it well.

- Ralph Waldo Emerson

Knowledge, which is divorced from justice, may be called cunning rather than wisdom.

- Marcus Tullius Cicero

We give advice, but we cannot give the wisdom to profit by it.

- Francois de La Rochefoucauld

Each of us finds his unique vehicle for sharing with others his bit of wisdom.

- Ram Dass

Wisdom has its root in goodness, not goodness its root in wisdom.

- Ralph Waldo Emerson

Cunning... is but the low mimic of wisdom.

- Plato

Gray hairs are signs of wisdom if you hold your tongue, speak and they are but hairs, as in the young.

- Rabindranath Tagore

Wisdom alone is the science of other sciences.

- Plato

The sum of wisdom is that time is never lost that is devoted to work.

- Ralph Waldo Emerson

The invariable mark of wisdom is to see the miraculous in the common.

- Ralph Waldo Emerson

Wisdom comes from within. Knowledge is acquired and can sometimes put a screen on your wisdom.

- A. R. Rahman

Some wisdom you must learn from one who's wise.

- Euripides

To keep your secret is wisdom; but to expect others to keep it is folly.

- Samuel Johnson

We can be knowledgeable with other men's knowledge but we cannot be wise with other men's wisdom.

- Michel de Montaigne

Much wisdom often goes with fewest words.

- Sophocles

If you were to offer a thirsty man all wisdom, you would not please him more than if you gave him a drink.

- Sophocles

I keep my friends as misers do their treasure, because, of all the things granted us by wisdom, none is greater or better than friendship.

- Pietro Aretino

I think it's nice to age gracefully. OK, you lose the youth, a certain stamina and dewy glow, but what you gain on the inside as a human being is wonderful: the wisdom, the acceptance and the peace of mind. It's a fair exchange.

- Cherie Lunghi

Sciences may be learned by rote, but wisdom not.

- **Laurence Sterne**

Wisdom is the abstract of the past, but beauty is the promise of the future.

- **Oliver Wendell Holmes, Sr.**

I actually don't think that I'm that much smarter than anybody else. It's just that I frequently just seem to know what to do, and I think that's wisdom.

- **Benjamin Carson**

In societies where mature workers are respected and where their wisdom is respected, everybody benefits. Workers are more engaged and productive. Their health is better. They live longer.

- **Deepak Chopra**

Without courage, wisdom bears no fruit.

- **Baltasar Gracian**

To know how to grow old is the master work of wisdom, and one of the most difficult chapters in the great art of living.

- **Herman Melville**

The seat of knowledge is in the head; of wisdom, in the heart. We are sure to judge wrong, if we do not feel right.

- William Hazlitt

The truest greatness lies in being kind, the truest wisdom in a happy mind.

- Ella Wheeler Wilcox

Never accept ultimatums, conventional wisdom, or absolutes.

- Christopher Reeve

Every speaker has a mouth;
An arrangement rather neat.
Sometimes it's filled with wisdom.
Sometimes it's filled with feet.

- Robert Orben

Men who know themselves are no longer fools. They stand on the threshold of the door of wisdom.

- Havelock Ellis

Our wisdom comes from our experience, and our experience comes from our foolishness.

- Sacha Guitry

Has fortune dealt you some bad cards? Then let wisdom make you a good gamester.

- **Francis Quarles**

The first point of wisdom is to discern that which is false; the second, to know that which is true.

- **Lactantius**

Authority without wisdom is like a heavy ax without an edge, fitter to bruise than polish.

- **Anne Bradstreet**

Wisdom oft times consists of knowing what to do next.

- **Herbert Hoover**

This society in which we live is radically changing. What previous generations saw as evil is now embraced as being good. It is a dangerous and slippery slope upon which we stand when we reject what Solomon called the beginning of wisdom - the fear of God.

- **Ray Comfort**

No one ever found wisdom without also being a fool. Writers, alas, have to be fools in public, while the rest of the human race can cover its tracks.

- Erica Jong

True wisdom listens more, talks less and can get along with all types of people.

- Kiana Tom

Wisdom is the knowledge of good and evil, not the strength to choose between the two.

- John Cheever

I'm now the elder in the position of doling out wisdom and trying to mend fences.

- Jane Fonda

The marvel of the Bhagavad-Gita is its truly beautiful revelation of life's wisdom which enables philosophy to blossom into religion.

- Herman Hesse

I have devoted my life to uncertainty. Certainty is the death of wisdom, thought, creativity.

- Shekhar Kapur

We live in a culture that doesn't acknowledge or validate human intuition and doesn't encourage us to rely on our intuitive wisdom.

- Shakti Gawain

If to live is to progress, if you are lucky, from foolishness to wisdom, then to write novels is to broadcast the various stages of your foolishness.

- Jane Smiley

However great an evil immorality may be, we must not forget that it is not without its beneficial consequences. It is only through extremes that men can arrive at the middle path of wisdom and virtue.

- Wilhelm von Humboldt

Sometimes one likes foolish people for their folly, better than wise people for their wisdom.

- Elizabeth Gaskell

In complete darkness, it is only knowledge and wisdom that separates us.

- Janet Jackson

One part of wisdom is knowing what you don't need anymore and letting it go.

- Jane Fonda

My past is my wisdom to use today... my future is my wisdom yet to experience. Be in the present because that is where life resides.

- Gene Oliver

Evil can be a teacher, if you look at the wisdom of its negative power.

- Tom Brown, Jr.

There's a real wisdom to not saying a thing.

- Willem Dafoe

Knowledge is a process of piling up facts; wisdom lies in their simplification.

- Martin H. Fischer

The greater the step forward in knowledge, the greater is the one taken backward in search of wisdom.

- Stephen Gardiner

The wisdom acquired with the passage of time is a useless gift unless you share it.

- **Esther Williams**

It isn't right to judge strength as better than good wisdom.

- **Xenophanes**

Sometimes you surprise yourself with what you can handle, and if you come out the other end with some wisdom, then it's not such a bad thing.

- **Boy George**

Where fear is present, wisdom cannot be.

- **Lactantius**

Unhappy is that Grandeur which makes us too great to be good; and that Wit which sets us at a distance from true Wisdom.

- **Mary Astell**

He, whose wisdom cannot help him, gets no good from being wise.

- **Quintus Ennius**

Pessimism is only the name that men of weak nerves give to wisdom.

- Bernard DeVoto

Silence and reserve will give anyone a reputation for wisdom.

- Myrtle Reed

I don't want to put a pause on the rest of my life; I'm really enjoying getting older and the wisdom that comes from that.

- Rosemarie DeWitt

The Divine wisdom has given us prayer, not as a means whereby to obtain the good things of earth, but as a means whereby we learn to do without them; not as a means whereby we escape evil, but as a means whereby we become strong to meet it.

- Frederick William Robertson

I feel increasingly like age is very irrelevant. Quite often, cynicism is confused with wisdom, and my scorn is confused with a knowing, which I don't have.

- Laura Marling

There is a trade off - as you grow older you gain wisdom but you lose spontaneity.

- **Kenny Rogers**

When you're used to being prepared to reject conventional wisdom, it leaves you open to learn more.

- **Mayim Bialik**

Memory is not wisdom; idiots can by rote repeat volumes. Yet what is wisdom without memory?

- **Martin Farquhar Tupper**

The most excellent and divine counsel, the best and most profitable advertisement of all others, but the least practiced, is to study and learn how to know ourselves. This is the foundation of wisdom and the highway to whatever is good.

- **Pierre Charron**

Knowledge is not just the preserve of the educated elite. Just because someone has not had a formal education, that does not mean he does not have wisdom and common sense.

- **Vikas Swarup**

Someday in the distant cyborg future, when our internal and external memories fully merge, we may come to possess infinite knowledge. But that's not the same thing as wisdom.

- **Joshua Foer**

If the highest things are unknowable, then the highest capacity or virtue of man cannot be theoretical wisdom.

- **Leo Strauss**

Wisdom is keeping a sense of fallibility of all our views and opinions.

- **Gerald Brenan**

You lose or you win the fight - and anything in life - in your mind. I can look at how the person walks, how he speaks, his expressions. It's a wisdom. Eyes are the mirror of the soul. So you can read a lot.

- **Wladimir Klitschko**

I'm exploring the maturity, the wisdom that just comes from having gone around the sun 50 times. My experience is, 'Oh, I'm never really going to get it right. I'm never going to get it done. But that's not the point here.' The point is the journey.

- **Melissa Etheridge**

I have sympathy for young people, for their growing pains, but I balk when these growing pains are pushed into the foreground, when you make these young people the only vehicles of life's wisdom.

- Wislawa Szymborska

Words of wisdom are spoken by children at least as often as scientists.

- James Newman

It is costly wisdom that is bought by experience.

- Roger Ascham

Christian, learn from Christ how you ought to love Christ. Learn a love that is tender, wise, strong; love with tenderness, not passion, wisdom, not foolishness, and strength, lest you become weary and turn away from the love of the Lord.

- Saint Bernard

For the Holy Ghost blesses us with optimism and wisdom at times of challenge that we simply cannot muster on our own.

- Sheri L. Dew

Books give not wisdom where none was before. But where some is, there reading makes it more.

- **Elizabeth Hardwick**

There is as much wisdom in listening as there is in speaking - and that goes for all relationships, not just romantic ones.

- **Daniel Dae Kim**

Man works outwardly and inwardly - after rest, he has energy; after energy, he needs repose; so, when we have given instruction for a time, we need instruction and must receive it, or the spirit faints and wisdom herself grows bitter.

- **James Stephens**

Wisdom denotes the pursuing of the best ends by the best means.

- **Francis Hutcheson**

Intelligence alone does not get us where we need to go or even necessarily where we want to go. For that, the human creature must exercise harder-won capacities of wisdom, and wise action.

- **Krista Tippett**

We dwell in the house of the body, but its perfection and intricate life are the work of a wisdom which never relaxes dominion over a single cell.

- George William Russell

Even youngish men can acquire wisdom as time goes by.

- John Bercow

I think there is a complicated side effect to overcoming evil in that we are forever changed by it. I think after we ingest some of the cruelty of the world, it takes years off of our lives, but it also gives us wisdom and a little grace, hopefully a sense of compassion.

- Adam Rapp

What I lack in energy, I have in wisdom.

- Marcia Cross

Genius unrefined resembles a flash of lightning, but wisdom is like the sun.

- Franz Grillparzer

Critical in this process of wisdom being passed down is that you also need to take it in; you need to listen to it.

- Andrew Zuckerman

This land, which we have watered with our tears and our blood, is now our mother country, and we are well satisfied to stay where wisdom abounds and gospel is free.

- Richard V. Allen

Practical wisdom is what's called for in situations that have a moral dimension to them.

- Barry Schwartz

I believe that when an elder dies, a library is burned: vast sums of wisdom and knowledge are lost. Throughout the world libraries are ablaze with scant attention.

- Elizabeth Kapu'uwailani Lindsey

To think ill of mankind and not wish ill to them, is perhaps the highest wisdom and virtue.

- William Hazlitt

Even when you have doubts, take that step. Take chances. Mistakes are never a failure - they can be turned into wisdom.

- Cat Cora

It is not white hair that engenders wisdom.

- Menander

Better than the strength of men and horses is our wisdom.

- **Xenophanes**

I do not believe in the collective wisdom of individual ignorance.

- **Thomas Carlyle**

The philosophical point is that our happiness and wellbeing is not based on incomes rising. This is not just the wisdom of sages but of ordinary people. Prosperity is more social and psychological: it's about identification, affiliation, participation in society and a sense of purpose.

- **Tim Jackson**

One could surely argue that the Buddhist tradition, taken as a whole, represents the richest source of contemplative wisdom that any civilization has produced.

- **Sam Harris**

For most of us, wisdom is acquired in the thicket of experience and usually meets us somewhere along the way if we live long enough. But sooner is better than later.

- **H. Jackson Brown, Jr.**

Knowledge is the consequence of time, and multitudes of days are fittest to teach wisdom.

- Jeremy Collier

It is astonishing what force, purity, and wisdom it requires for a human being to keep clear of falsehoods.

- Margaret Fuller

Along with success comes a reputation for wisdom.

- Euripides

I don't think you can come into your wisdom until you have made mistakes on your own skin and felt them in reality of your own life.

- Elizabeth Gilbert

When I was at drama school, I wanted to change the world, and thought I had some great wisdom to impart to people about humanity. Now that I'm older, I know enough to realise that I know nothing at all.

- Michael Sheen

The 'wisdom of the crowds' is the most ridiculous statement I've heard in my life. Crowds are dumb.

- Drew Curtis

A short saying often contains much wisdom.

- **Sophocles**

It is the province of knowledge to speak, and it is the privilege of wisdom to listen.

- **Oliver Wendell Holmes, Sr.**

One of the greatest pieces of economic wisdom is to know what you do not know.

- **John Kenneth Galbraith**

Young people, you need the wisdom of age, just as some of us older ones need your enthusiasm for life.

- **Ezra Taft Benson**

Our experience is composed rather of illusions lost than of wisdom acquired.

- **Joseph Roux**

That which seems the height of absurdity in one generation often becomes the height of wisdom in another.

- **Adlai E. Stevenson**

Lessons of wisdom have the most power over us when they capture the heart through the groundwork of a story, which engages the passions.

- Laurence Sterne

The enemy of the conventional wisdom is not ideas but the march of events.

- John Kenneth Galbraith

The hunger for facile wisdom is the root of all false philosophy.

- George Santayana

Wisdom is knowledge which has become a part of one's being.

- Orison Swett Marden

Wisdom has never made a bigot, but learning has.

- Josh Billings

It is good even for old men to learn wisdom.

- Aeschylus

The wisdom of age: don't stop walking.

- **Mason Cooley**

Wisdom is humble that he knows no more.

- **William Cowper**

They would need to be already wise, in order to love wisdom.

- **Friedrich Schiller**

Wisdom consists not so much in knowing what to do in the ultimate as knowing what to do next.

- **Herbert Hoover**

We all admire the wisdom of people who come to us for advice.

- **Arthur Helps**

Lord, give us the wisdom to utter words that are gentle and tender, for tomorrow we may have to eat them.

- **Mo Udall**

Knowledge is marvellous, but wisdom is even better.

- **Kay Redfield Jamison**

You can practice to attain knowledge, but you can't practice to attain wisdom.

- Herbie Hancock

Wisdom alone is true ambition's aim,
Wisdom is the source of virtue and of fame;
Obtained with labour, for mankind employed,
And then, when most you share it, best enjoyed.

- Alfred North Whitehead

The wisdom and experience of older people is a resource of inestimable worth. Recognizing and treasuring the contributions of older people is essential to the long-term flourishing of any society.

- Daisaku Ikeda

Wisdom not only gets, but once got, retains.

- Francis Quarles

If I can turn the most powerful part of the world into a land of wisdom and compassion, it's going to change the rest of the world.

- Chade-Meng Tan

All free governments are managed by the combined wisdom and folly of the people.

- James A. Garfield

Wisdom lies neither in fixity nor in change, but in the dialectic between the two.

- Octavio Paz

Full of wisdom are the ordinations of fate.

- Friedrich Schiller

We have no words for speaking of wisdom to the stupid. He who understands the wise is wise already.

- Georg C. Lichtenberg

Knowledge shrinks as wisdom grows.

- Alfred North Whitehead

Government is a contrivance of human wisdom to provide for human wants. People have the right to expect that these wants will be provided for by this wisdom.

- Jimmy Carter

The clouds may drop down titles and estates, and wealth may seek us, but wisdom must be sought.

- Edward Young

It is almost everywhere the case that soon after it is begotten the greater part of human wisdom is laid to rest in repositories.

- Georg C. Lichtenberg

Wisdom is not acquired save as the result of investigation.

- Sara Teasdale

Wisdom may best arise from a humbling reality.

- Michael Leunig

Without wisdom, the future has no meaning, no valuable purpose.

- Herbie Hancock

The beginning of wisdom is to desire it.

- Solomon Ibn Gabirol

The sublimity of wisdom is to do those things living, which are to be desired when dying.

- Norman Douglas

How do you rate works of genius? Partly by personal inclination, partly by accepted wisdom, partly by popularity.

- Robert Gottlieb

We all have within us a deep wisdom, but sometimes we don't know we have it.

- Shakti Gawain

Wisdom is knowing when you can't be wise.

- Paul Engle

I look at being older and gaining wisdom. I've learned to stay fit and healthy. I accept my body, my life, and my circumstances.

- Kim Alexis

Instead of looking at life as a narrowing funnel, we can see it ever widening to choose the things we want to do, to take the wisdom we've learned and create something.

- Liz Carpenter

Doubt the conventional wisdom unless you can verify it with reason and experiment.

- Steve Albini

Now it is time to turn to an older wisdom that, while respecting material comfort and security as a basic right of all, also recognises that many of the most valuable things in life cannot be measured.

- Michael D. Higgins

Be there a will, and wisdom finds a way.

- George Crabbe

Contemplation and wisdom are highest achievements and man is not totally at home with them.

- Gabriel Marcel

Though I am fascinated by knowledge, I am even more fascinated by wisdom.

- Abraham Verghese

Wisdom prepares for the worst, but folly leaves the worst for the day when it comes.

- Richard Cecil

Wisdom is a kind of knowledge. It is knowledge of the nature, career, and consequences of human values.

- Sidney Hook

The problem lies with us: we've become addicted to experts. We've become addicted to their certainty, their assuredness, their definitiveness, and in the process, we have ceded our responsibility, substituting our intellect and our intelligence for their supposed words of wisdom.

- Noreena Hertz

Women are stronger than men - they do not die of wisdom.

- James Stephens

A proverb is the wisdom of many and the wit of one.

- Lord John Russell

With age comes a greater wisdom, an ease and comfort with oneself.

- Cherie Lunghi

I actually think with age comes some level of wisdom.

- Nina Totenberg

Normally street children are shown in terms of the tragedy of their lives - which is true - but there's also another dimension: their wisdom, dignity and enormous capacity for survival.

- Henning Mankell

Wisdom too often never comes, and so one ought not to reject it merely because it comes late.

- Felix Frankfurter

Your aim will be knowledge and wisdom, not the reflected glamour of fame.

- Abbott L. Lowell

Peace is a fragile thing. It takes courage to secure it. It takes wisdom to maintain it.

- Jenny Shipley

I'm not a money manager, but I can tell you what the conventional wisdom is. The younger you are, the more risk you can take on.

- Maria Bartiromo

Books should to one of these fours ends conduce, for wisdom, piety, delight, or use.

- John Denham

If people can't acknowledge the wisdom of indigenous cultures, then that's their loss.

- Jay Griffiths

I left school at 16 but I wish I'd gone to university - I think I would have studied English literature. I had a knack for that. But I don't think you have the kind of wisdom at 16 to make that decision.

- Brendan Coyle

You need to have extraordinary wisdom to be the forerunner.

- Ma Huateng

In order to enjoy your own life, you need to be good to everyone all of the time.

- Robert Jamgotchian

Success

Mistakes are the stepping-stones and the corner stone of success.

- Vahan Chanakian

Success consists of going from failure to failure without loss of enthusiasm.

- Winston Churchill

I've failed over and over and over again in my life and that is why I succeed.

- Michael Jordan

Success is a wonderful thing, but it tends not to be the sort of experience that we learn from. We enjoy it; perhaps we even deserve it. But we don't acquire wisdom from it.

- Timothy Noah

Success is not final, failure is not fatal: it is the courage to continue that counts.

- Winston Churchill

The price of success is hard work, dedication to the job at hand, and the determination that whether we win or lose, we have applied the best of ourselves to the task at hand.

- Vince Lombardi

To succeed in life, you need two things: ignorance and confidence.

- Mark Twain

Coming together is a beginning; keeping together is progress; working together is success.

- Henry Ford

The starting point of all achievement is desire.

- Napoleon Hill

Don't aim for success if you want it; just do what you love and believe in, and it will come naturally.

- David Frost

Try not to become a man of success, but rather try to become a man of value.

- Albert Einstein

Desire is the key to motivation, but it's determination and commitment to an unrelenting pursuit of your goal - a commitment to excellence - that will enable you to attain the success you seek.

- Mario Andretti

Take up one idea. Make that one idea your life - think of it, dream of it, live on that idea. Let the brain, muscles, nerves, every part of your body, be full of that idea, and just leave every other idea alone. This is the way to success.

- Swami Vivekananda

Success is not the key to happiness. Happiness is the key to success. If you love what you are doing, you will be successful.

- Albert Schweitzer

A successful man is one who can lay a firm foundation with the bricks others have thrown at him.

- David Brinkley

Success makes so many people hate you. I wish it wasn't that way. It would be wonderful to enjoy success without seeing envy in the eyes of those around you.

- Marilyn Monroe

The difference between a successful person and others is not a lack of strength, not a lack of knowledge, but rather a lack of will.

- Vince Lombardi

Think twice before you speak, because your words and influence will plant the seed of either success or failure in the mind of another.

- Napoleon Hill

Formal education will make you a living; self-education will make you a fortune.

- Jim Rohn

Happiness lies in the joy of achievement and the thrill of creative effort.

- Franklin D. Roosevelt

Success is a lousy teacher. It seduces smart people into thinking they can't lose.

- Bill Gates

If everyone is moving forward together, then success takes care of itself.

- Henry Ford

In order to succeed, your desire for success should be greater than your fear of failure.

- **Bill Cosby**

I don't measure a man's success by how high he climbs but how high he bounces when he hits bottom.

- **George S. Patton**

No man succeeds without a good woman behind him. Wife or mother, if it is both, he is twice blessed indeed.

- **Godfrey Winn**

Success depends upon previous preparation, and without such preparation there is sure to be failure.

- **Confucius**

It had long since come to my attention that people of accomplishment rarely sat back and let things happen to them. They went out and happened to things.

- **Leonardo da Vinci**

The foundation stones for a balanced success are honesty, character, integrity, faith, love and loyalty.

- **Zig Ziglar**

Action is the foundational key to all success.

- Pablo Picasso

Always bear in mind that your own resolution to succeed is more important than any other.

- Abraham Lincoln

Success is peace of mind which is a direct result of self-satisfaction in knowing you did your best to become the best you are capable of becoming.

- John Wooden

Act, look, feel successful, conduct yourself accordingly, and you will be amazed at the positive results.

- William James

Success is not measured by what you accomplish, but by the opposition you have encountered, and the courage with which you have maintained the struggle against overwhelming odds.

- Orison Swett Marden

If you have no critics you'll likely have no success.

- Malcolm X

The size of your success is measured by the strength of your desire; the size of your dream; and how you handle disappointment along the way.

- Robert Kiyosaki

The secret of my success is a two-word answer: Know people.

- Harvey S. Firestone

The most important single ingredient in the formula of success is knowing how to get along with people.

- Theodore Roosevelt

When love and skill work together, expect a masterpiece.

- John Ruskin

Success is simple. Do what's right, the right way, at the right time.

- Arnold H. Glasow

Success comes from knowing that you did your best to become the best that you are capable of becoming.

- John Wooden

The greatest sign of success for a teacher... is to be able to say, 'The children are now working as if I did not exist.'
- Maria Montessori

There is little success where there is little laughter.
- Andrew Carnegie

I have learned that success is to be measured not so much by the position that one has reached in life as by the obstacles which he has had to overcome while trying to succeed.
- Booker T. Washington

Success isn't measured by money or power or social rank. Success is measured by your discipline and inner peace.
- Mike Ditka

If you want to be truly successful invest in yourself to get the knowledge you need to find your unique factor. When you find it and focus on it and persevere, your success will blossom.
- Sydney Madwed

To be prepared is half the victory.
- Miguel de Cervantes

Eighty percent of success in life is showing up.

- Woody Allen

Success is not forever and failure isn't fatal.

- Don Shula

Frustration, although quite painful at times, is a very positive and essential part of success.

- Bo Bennett

The successful man will profit from his mistakes and try again in a different way.

- Dale Carnegie

Failure is not an option. Everyone has to succeed.

- Arnold Schwarzenegger

Winning isn't everything, it's the only thing.

- Vince Lombardi

The ladder of success is best climbed by stepping on the rungs of opportunity.

- Ayn Rand

A champion is afraid of losing. Everyone else is afraid of winning.

- Billie Jean King

Whosoever desires constant success must change his conduct with the times.

- Niccolo Machiavelli

Success is not a good teacher, failure makes you humble.

- Shahrukh Khan

Develop success from failures. Discouragement and failure are two of the surest stepping-stones to success.

- Dale Carnegie

Once you agree upon the price you and your family must pay for success, it enables you to ignore the minor hurts, the opponent's pressure, and the temporary failures.

- Vince Lombardi

Success is dependent on effort.

- Sophocles

There is no success without hardship.

- Sophocles

It is no use saying, 'We are doing our best.' You have got to succeed in doing what is necessary.

- Winston Churchill

Man needs his difficulties because they are necessary to enjoy success.

- A. P. J. Abdul Kalam

What is success? I think it is a mixture of having a flair for the thing that you are doing; knowing that it is not enough, that you have got to have hard work and a certain sense of purpose.

- Margaret Thatcher

Success is falling nine times and getting up ten.

- Jon Bon Jovi

One secret of success in life is for a man to be ready for his opportunity when it comes.

- Benjamin Disraeli

The real secret of success is enthusiasm.

                                        - Walter Chrysler

Success has a simple formula: do your best, and people may like it.

                                          - Sam Ewing

To be successful, you have to have your heart in your business and your business in your heart.

                                          - Thomas J. Watson

Much effort, much prosperity.

                                          - Euripides

Flaming enthusiasm, backed up by horse sense and persistence, is the quality that most frequently makes for success.

                                          - Dale Carnegie

Success is blocked by concentrating on it and planning for it... Success is shy - it won't come out while you're watching.

                                          - Tennessee Williams

I don't know the key to success, but the key to failure is trying to please everybody.

- Bill Cosby

Success is a science; if you have the conditions, you get the result.

- Oscar Wilde

They succeed, because they think they can.

- Virgil

Success is getting what you want. Happiness is wanting what you get.

- Dale Carnegie

Belief in oneself is one of the most important bricks in building any successful venture.

- Lydia M. Child

The one thing that I know is that you win with good people.

- Don Shula

Success isn't a result of spontaneous combustion. You must set yourself on fire.

- Arnold H. Glasow

The thermometer of success is merely the jealousy of the malcontents.

- Salvador Dali

Success is finding satisfaction in giving a little more than you take.

- Christopher Reeve

Success consists of getting up just one more time than you fall.

- Oliver Goldsmith

Most people give up just when they're about to achieve success. They quit on the one-yard line. They give up at the last minute of the game one-foot from a winning touchdown.

- Ross Perot

Failure is success if we learn from it.

- Malcolm Forbes

The five essential entrepreneurial skills for success: Concentration, Discrimination, Organization, Innovation and Communication.

- Harold S. Geneen

Diligence is the mother of good fortune.

- Benjamin Disraeli

The secrets of success are a good wife and a steady job. My wife told me.

- Howard Nemerov

Success is often the result of taking a misstep in the right direction.

- Al Bernstein

The common idea that success spoils people by making them vain, egotistic and self-complacent is erroneous; on the contrary it makes them, for the most part, humble, tolerant and kind.

- W. Somerset Maugham

I honestly think it is better to be a failure at something you love than to be a success at something you hate.

- George Burns

The measure of success is not whether you have a tough problem to deal with, but whether it is the same problem you had last year.

- John Foster Dulles

Defeat is not the worst of failures. Not to have tried is the true failure.

- George Edward Woodberry

How can they say my life is not a success? Have I not for more than sixty years got enough to eat and escaped being eaten?

- Logan Pearsall Smith

The toughest thing about success is that you've got to keep on being a success.

- Irving Berlin

Do something you really like, and hopefully it pays the rent. As far as I'm concerned, that's success.

- Tom Petty

The secret of success is sincerity.

- Jean Giraudoux

Success is the child of drudgery and perseverance. It cannot be coaxed or bribed; pay the price and it is yours.

- Orison Swett Marden

Success is the progressive realization of predetermined, worthwhile, personal goals.

- Paul J. Meyer

Success in almost any field depends more on energy and drive than it does on intelligence. This explains why we have so many stupid leaders.

- Sloan Wilson

Success breeds success.

- Mia Hamm

Winning isn't everything, but it beats anything in second place.

- William C. Bryant

We fall forward to succeed.

- Mary Kay Ash

When you win, nothing hurts.

- **Joe Namath**

Success seems to be largely a matter of hanging on after others have let go.

- **William Feather**

In order to succeed you must fail, so that you know what not to do the next time.

- **Anthony J. D'Angelo**

To design the future effectively, you must first let go of your past.

- **Charles J. Givens**

Pray that success will not come any faster than you are able to endure it.

- **Elbert Hubbard**

In this world it is not what we take up, but what we give up, that makes us rich.

- **Henry Ward Beecher**

Definiteness of purpose is the starting point of all achievement.

- W. Clement Stone

To know even one life has breathed easier because you have lived. This is to have succeeded.

- Bessie Anderson Stanley

The man who has done his level best... is a success, even though the world may write him down a failure.

- B. C. Forbes

Nothing succeeds like success.

- Alexandre Dumas

He has achieved success who has worked well, laughed often, and loved much.

- Elbert Hubbard

Prospering just doesn't have to do with money.

- Joel Osteen

It's our nature: Human beings like success but they hate successful people.

- Carrot Top

The one phrase you can use is that success has a thousand fathers, and failure is an orphan.

- Alan Price

I don't think about financial success as the measurement of my success.

- Christie Hefner

Put your heart, mind, and soul into even your smallest acts. This is the secret of success.

- Swami Sivananda

There are no secrets to success. It is the result of preparation, hard work, and learning from failure.

- Colin Powell

The season of failure is the best time for sowing the seeds of success.

- Paramahansa Yogananda

Character cannot be developed in ease and quiet. Only through experience of trial and suffering can the soul be strengthened, ambition inspired, and success achieved.

- Helen Keller

Education is the key to success in life, and teachers make a lasting impact in the lives of their students.

- Solomon Ortiz

It's fine to celebrate success but it is more important to heed the lessons of failure.

- Bill Gates

Without continual growth and progress, such words as improvement, achievement, and success have no meaning.

- Benjamin Franklin

The way a team plays as a whole determines its success. You may have the greatest bunch of individual stars in the world, but if they don't play together, the club won't be worth a dime.

- Babe Ruth

Humility is the true key to success. Successful people lose their way at times. They often embrace and overindulge from the fruits of success. Humility halts this arrogance and self-indulging trap. Humble people share the credit and wealth, remaining focused and hungry to continue the journey of success.

- Rick Pitino

We learned about honesty and integrity - that the truth matters... that you don't take shortcuts or play by your own set of rules... and success doesn't count unless you earn it fair and square.

- Michelle Obama

Success is not a destination, but the road that you're on. Being successful means that you're working hard and walking your walk every day. You can only live your dream by working hard towards it. That's living your dream.

- Marlon Wayans

The supreme quality for leadership is unquestionably integrity. Without it, no real success is possible, no matter whether it is on a section gang, a football field, in an army, or in an office.

- Dwight D. Eisenhower

At the end of the day, you are solely responsible for your success and your failure. And the sooner you realize that, you accept that, and integrate that into your work ethic, you will start being successful. As long as you blame others for the reason you aren't where you want to be, you will always be a failure.

- Erin Cummings

At the end of the day, the most overwhelming key to a child's success is the positive involvement of parents.

- Jane D. Hull

I attribute my success to this - I never gave or took any excuse.

- Florence Nightingale

A little more persistence, a little more effort, and what seemed hopeless failure may turn to glorious success.

- Elbert Hubbard

Communication - the human connection - is the key to personal and career success.

- Paul J. Meyer

Focused, hard work is the real key to success. Keep your eyes on the goal, and just keep taking the next step towards completing it. If you aren't sure which way to do something, do it both ways and see which works better.

- John Carmack

Before anything else, preparation is the key to success.

- Alexander Graham Bell

My success was due to good luck, hard work, and support and advice from friends and mentors. But most importantly, it depended on me to keep trying after I had failed.

- Mark Warner

Success is where preparation and opportunity meet.

- Bobby Unser

Ambition is the path to success. Persistence is the vehicle you arrive in.

- Bill Bradley

Many of life's failures are people who did not realize how close they were to success when they gave up.

- Thomas A. Edison

If one advances confidently in the direction of his dreams, and endeavors to live the life which he has imagined, he will meet with a success unexpected in common hours.

- Henry David Thoreau

Honesty and loyalty are key. If two people can be honest with each other about everything, that's probably the biggest key to success.

- Taylor Lautner

Fear can be good when you're walking past an alley at night or when you need to check the locks on your doors before you go to bed, but it's not good when you have a goal and you're fearful of obstacles. We often get trapped by our fears, but anyone who has had success has failed before.

- Queen Latifah

Patience, persistence and perspiration make an unbeatable combination for success.

- Napoleon Hill

Success is not built on success. It's built on failure. It's built on frustration. Sometimes its built on catastrophe.

- Sumner Redstone

Failure is the key to success; each mistake teaches us something.

- Morihei Ueshiba

For success, attitude is equally as important as ability.

- Walter Scott

One important key to success is self-confidence. An important key to self-confidence is preparation.

- Arthur Ashe

Success comes to those who dedicate everything to their passion in life. To be successful, it is also very important to be humble and never let fame or money travel to your head.

- A. R. Rahman

If you want to succeed you should strike out on new paths, rather than travel the worn paths of accepted success.

- John D. Rockefeller

No one succeeds without effort... Those who succeed owe their success to perseverance.

- Ramana Maharshi

We learned about gratitude and humility - that so many people had a hand in our success, from the teachers who inspired us to the janitors who kept our school clean... and we were taught to value everyone's contribution and treat everyone with respect.

- Michelle Obama

The secret of success is learning how to use pain and pleasure instead of having pain and pleasure use you. If you do that, you're in control of your life. If you don't, life controls you.

- Tony Robbins

Desire is the key to motivation, but it's the determination and commitment to unrelenting pursuit of your goal - a commitment to excellence - that will enable you to attain the success you seek.

- Mario Andretti

I know of no single formula for success. But over the years I have observed that some attributes of leadership are universal and are often about finding ways of encouraging people to combine their efforts, their talents, their insights, their enthusiasm and their inspiration to work together.

- Queen Elizabeth II

A strong, positive self-image is the best possible preparation for success.

- Joyce Brothers

We all learn lessons in life. Some stick, some don't. I have always learned more from rejection and failure than from acceptance and success.

- Henry Rollins

The dictionary is the only place that success comes before work. Hard work is the price we must pay for success. I think you can accomplish anything if you're willing to pay the price.

- Vince Lombardi

Your success and happiness lies in you. Resolve to keep happy, and your joy and you shall form an invincible host against difficulties.

- Helen Keller

We were all born with a certain degree of power. The key to success is discovering this innate power and using it daily to deal with whatever challenges come our way.

- Les Brown

You cannot climb the ladder of success dressed in the costume of failure.

- Zig Ziglar

Success is the sum of small efforts - repeated day in and day out.

- Robert Collier

You wanna know what scares people? Success. When you don't make moves and when you don't climb up the ladder, everybody loves you because you're not competition.

- Nicki Minaj

Success is only meaningful and enjoyable if it feels like your own.

- Michelle Obama

True success is overcoming the fear of being unsuccessful.

- Paul Sweeney

The best revenge is massive success.

- Frank Sinatra

You are a product of your environment. So choose the environment that will best develop you toward your objective. Analyze your life in terms of its environment. Are the things around you helping you toward success - or are they holding you back?

— W. Clement Stone

Willpower is the key to success. Successful people strive no matter what they feel by applying their will to overcome apathy, doubt or fear.

— Dan Millman

Success comes from taking the initiative and following up... persisting... eloquently expressing the depth of your love. What simple action could you take today to produce a new momentum toward success in your life?

— Tony Robbins

The making of friends who are real friends, is the best token we have of a man's success in life.

— Edward Everett Hale

Success does not consist in never making mistakes but in never making the same one a second time.

— George Bernard Shaw

Procrastination is one of the most common and deadliest of diseases and its toll on success and happiness is heavy.

- Wayne Gretzky

Life is a series of punches. It presents a lot of challenges. It presents a lot of hardship, but the people that are able to take those punches and able to move forward are the ones that really do have a lot of success and have a lot of joy in their life and have a lot of stories to tell, too.

- Josh Turner

Before success comes in any man's life, he's sure to meet with much temporary defeat and, perhaps some failures. When defeat overtakes a man, the easiest and the most logical thing to do is to quit. That's exactly what the majority of men do.

- Napoleon Hill

No student ever attains very eminent success by simply doing what is required of him: it is the amount and excellence of what is over and above the required, that determines the greatness of ultimate distinction.

- Charles Kendall Adams

The key to success is to focus our conscious mind on things we desire not things we fear.

- Brian Tracy

I do not think that there is any other quality so essential to success of any kind as the quality of perseverance. It overcomes almost everything, even nature.

- John D. Rockefeller

Our goals can only be reached through a vehicle of a plan, in which we must fervently believe, and upon which we must vigorously act. There is no other route to success.

- Pablo Picasso

Our daily decisions and habits have a huge impact upon both our levels of happiness and success.

- Shawn Achor

Learning and innovation go hand in hand. The arrogance of success is to think that what you did yesterday will be sufficient for tomorrow.

- William Pollard

Success is peace of mind, which is a direct result of self-satisfaction in knowing you made the effort to become the best of which you are capable.

- John Wooden

The secret of our success is that we never, never give up.

- Wilma Mankiller

Through perseverance many people win success out of what seemed destined to be certain failure.

- Benjamin Disraeli

Let us realize that: the privilege to work is a gift, the power to work is a blessing, the love of work is success!

- David O. McKay

Money and success don't change people; they merely amplify what is already there.

- Will Smith

Perseverance is a great element of success. If you only knock long enough and loud enough at the gate, you are sure to wake up somebody.

- Henry Wadsworth Longfellow

The definition of success to me is not necessarily a price tag, not fame, but having a good life, and being able to say I did the right thing at the end of the day.

- Jeremy Luke

The path to success is to take massive, determined action.

- **Tony Robbins**

I'm an addict, I'm addicted to success. Thankfully, there's no rehab for success.

- **Lil Wayne**

Success is never final, failure is never fatal. It's courage that counts.

- **John Wooden**

If there is any one secret of success, it lies in the ability to get the other person's point of view and see things from that person's angle as well as from your own.

- **Henry Ford**

Part of being a man is learning to take responsibility for your successes and for your failures. You can't go blaming others or being jealous. Seeing somebody else's success as your failure is a cancerous way to live.

- **Kevin Bacon**

Think little goals and expect little achievements. Think big goals and win big success.

- **David Joseph Schwartz**

Good planning is important. I've also regarded a sense of humor as one of the most important things on a big expedition. When you're in a difficult or dangerous situation, or when you're depressed about the chances of success, someone who can make you laugh eases the tension.

- Edmund Hillary

Honesty and integrity are absolutely essential for success in life - all areas of life. The really good news is that anyone can develop both honesty and integrity.

- Zig Ziglar

Success is a journey, not a destination. The doing is often more important than the outcome.

- Arthur Ashe

Ambition is the path to success; persistence is the vehicle you arrive in.

- William Eardley IV

Like success, failure is many things to many people. With Positive Mental Attitude, failure is a learning experience, a rung on the ladder, a plateau at which to get your thoughts in order and prepare to try again.

- W. Clement Stone

The level of our success is limited only by our imagination and no act of kindness, however small, is ever wasted.

- Aesop

If you work just for money, you'll never make it, but if you love what you're doing and you always put the customer first, success will be yours.

- Ray Kroc

The secret of your success is determined by your daily agenda.

- John C. Maxwell

Four things for success: work and pray, think and believe.

- Norman Vincent Peale

No one who achieves success does so without acknowledging the help of others. The wise and confident acknowledge this help with gratitude.

- Alfred North Whitehead

My success was not based so much on any great intelligence but on great common sense.

- Helen Gurley Brown

There is simply no substitute for hard work when it comes to achieving success.

- Heather Bresch

I don't take success and failure seriously. The only thing I do seriously is march forward. If I fall, I get up and march again.

- Kareena Kapoor Khan

Success is neither magical nor mysterious. Success is the natural consequence of consistently applying the basic fundamentals.

- Jim Rohn

Those who cannot work with their hearts achieve but a hollow, half-hearted success that breeds bitterness all around.

- A. P. J. Abdul Kalam

Never continue in a job you don't enjoy. If you're happy in what you're doing, you'll like yourself, you'll have inner peace. And if you have that, along with physical health, you will have had more success than you could possibly have imagined.

- Johnny Carson

Never lose sight of the fact that the most important yardstick of your success will be how you treat other people - your family, friends, and co-workers, and even strangers you meet along the way.

- Barbara Bush

Success seems to be connected with action. Successful people keep moving. They make mistakes, but they don't quit.

- Conrad Hilton

The most glorious moments in your life are not the so-called days of success, but rather those days when out of dejection and despair you feel rise in you a challenge to life, and the promise of future accomplishments.

- Gustave Flaubert

The foundation of success in life is good health: that is the substratum fortune; it is also the basis of happiness. A person cannot accumulate a fortune very well when he is sick.

- P. T. Barnum

Nothing succeeds like the appearance of success.

- Christopher Lasch

I believe that being successful means having a balance of success stories across the many areas of your life. You can't truly be considered successful in your business life if your home life is in shambles.

- Zig Ziglar

Obstacles are necessary for success because in selling, as in all careers of importance, victory comes only after many struggles and countless defeats.

- Og Mandino

That should be the measure of success for everyone. It's not money, it's not fame, it's not celebrity; my index of success is happiness.

- Lupe Fiasco

People talk about bullying, but you can be your own bully in some ways. You can be the person who is standing in the way of your success, and that was the case for me.

- Katy Perry

A rejection is nothing more than a necessary step in the pursuit of success.

- Bo Bennett

Success represents the 1% of your work which results from the 99% that is called failure.

- Soichiro Honda

An empowered organisation is one in which individuals have the knowledge, skill, desire, and opportunity to personally succeed in a way that leads to collective organisational success.

- Stephen Covey

The only way to permanently change the temperature in the room is to reset the thermostat. In the same way, the only way to change your level of financial success 'permanently' is to reset your financial thermostat. But it is your choice whether you choose to change.

- T. Harv Eker

What material success does is provide you with the ability to concentrate on other things that really matter. And that is being able to make a difference, not only in your own life, but in other people's lives.

- Oprah Winfrey

Your positive action combined with positive thinking results in success.

- Shiv Khera

Enjoying success requires the ability to adapt. Only by being open to change will you have a true opportunity to get the most from your talent.

- Nolan Ryan

The moment we believe that success is determined by an ingrained level of ability as opposed to resilience and hard work, we will be brittle in the face of adversity.

- Joshua Waitzkin

No matter how much success you're having, you can't continue working together if you can't communicate.

- Matt Cameron

We need to accept that we won't always make the right decisions, that we'll screw up royally sometimes - understanding that failure is not the opposite of success, it's part of success.

- Arianna Huffington

Self-belief and hard work will always earn you success.

- Virat Kohli

The road to success is always under construction.

- Lily Tomlin

Commitment, belief and positive attitude are all important if you're going to be a success, whether you're in sports, in business or, as in my case, anthropology.

- Donald Johanson

The battle of life is, in most cases, fought uphill; and to win it without a struggle were perhaps to win it without honor. If there were no difficulties there would be no success; if there were nothing to struggle for, there would be nothing to be achieved.

- Samuel Smiles

Success without honor is an unseasoned dish; it will satisfy your hunger, but it won't taste good.

- Joe Paterno

Success is having to worry about every damn thing in the world, except money.

- Johnny Cash

Some of the best lessons we ever learn are learned from past mistakes. The error of the past is the wisdom and success of the future.

- Dale Turner

That some achieve great success is proof to all that others can achieve it as well.

- Abraham Lincoln

Success means having the courage, the determination, and the will to become the person you believe you were meant to be.

- George A. Sheehan

Success is not a function of the size of your title but the richness of your contribution.

- Robin S. Sharma

Failure is only postponed success as long as courage 'coaches' ambition. The habit of persistence is the habit of victory.

- Herbert Kaufman

Nothing good comes in life or athletics unless a lot of hard work has preceded the effort. Only temporary success is achieved by taking short cuts.

- Roger Staubach

The winner's edge is not in a gifted birth, a high IQ, or in talent. The winner's edge is all in the attitude, not aptitude. Attitude is the criterion for success.

- Denis Waitley

Your success depends mainly upon what you think of yourself and whether you believe in yourself.

- William J. H. Boetcker

That man is a success who has lived well, laughed often and loved much.

- Robert Louis Stevenson

The more tranquil a man becomes, the greater is his success, his influence, his power for good. Calmness of mind is one of the beautiful jewels of wisdom.

- James Allen

What strikes me is that there's a very fine line between success and failure. Just one ingredient can make the difference.

- Andrew Lloyd Webber

In all our deeds, the proper value and respect for time determines success or failure.

- Malcolm X

Success is achieved by developing our strengths, not by eliminating our weaknesses.

- Marilyn vos Savant

Any fact facing us is not as important as our attitude toward it, for that determines our success or failure. The way you think about a fact may defeat you before you ever do anything about it. You are overcome by the fact because you think you are.

- Norman Vincent Peale

For true success ask yourself these four questions: Why? Why not? Why not me? Why not now?

- James Allen

Whenever you have taken up work in hand, you must see it to the finish. That is the ultimate secret of success. Never, never, never give up!

- Dada Vaswani

Success in life is founded upon attention to the small things rather than to the large things; to the every day things nearest to us rather than to the things that are remote and uncommon.

- Booker T. Washington

Success is due to our stretching to the challenges of life. Failure comes when we shrink from them.

- John C. Maxwell

Success is getting what you want. Happiness is liking what you get.

- H. Jackson Brown, Jr.

Try to look at your weakness and convert it into your strength. That's success.

- Zig Ziglar

You can be discouraged by failure, or you can learn from it. So go ahead and make mistakes, make all you can. Because, remember that's where you'll find success - on the far side of failure.

- Thomas J. Watson

Think of success as a game of chance in which you have control over the odds. As you begin to master concepts in personal achievement, you are increasing your odds of achieving success.

- Bo Bennett

I've had great success being a total idiot.

- Jerry Lewis

As my father used to tell me, the only true sign of success in life is being able to do for a living that which makes you happy.

- Al Yankovic

Success is steady progress toward one's personal goals.

- Jim Rohn

Success is nothing if you don't have the right people to share it with; you're just gonna end up lonely.

- Selena Gomez

I always say be humble but be firm. Humility and openness are the key to success without compromising your beliefs.

- George Hickenlooper

Have regular hours for work and play; make each day both useful and pleasant, and prove that you understand the worth of time by employing it well. Then youth will be delightful, old age will bring few regrets, and life will become a beautiful success.

- Louisa May Alcott

Nothing succeeds like success. Get a little success, and then just get a little more.

- Maya Angelou

I owe my success to having listened respectfully to the very best advice, and then going away and doing the exact opposite.

- Gilbert K. Chesterton

The new midlife is where you realize that even your failures make you more beautiful and are turned spiritually into success if you became a better person because of them. You became a more humble person. You became a more merciful and compassionate person.

- Marianne Williamson

Failure is the condiment that gives success its flavor.

- Truman Capote

One might think that the money value of an invention constitutes its reward to the man who loves his work. But... I continue to find my greatest pleasure, and so my reward, in the work that precedes what the world calls success.

- Thomas A. Edison

Every person who wins in any undertaking must be willing to cut all sources of retreat. Only by doing so can one be sure of maintaining that state of mind known as a burning desire to win - essential to success.

- Napoleon Hill

The two most important requirements for major success are: first, being in the right place at the right time, and second, doing something about it.

- Ray Kroc

Ego stops you from getting things done and getting people to work with you. That's why I firmly believe that ego and success are not compatible.

- Harvey Mackay

I can't imagine a person becoming a success who doesn't give this game of life everything he's got.

- Walter Cronkite

I must admit that I personally measure success in terms of the contributions an individual makes to her or his fellow human beings.

- **Margaret Mead**

The penalty of success is to be bored by people who used to snub you.

- **Nancy Astor**

Success in its highest and noblest form calls for peace of mind and enjoyment and happiness which come only to the man who has found the work that he likes best.

- **Napoleon Hill**

Nobody travels on the road to success without a puncture or two.

- **Navjot Singh Sidhu**

My success just evolved from working hard at the business at hand each day.

- **Johnny Carson**

The only question to ask yourself is, how much are you willing to sacrifice to achieve this success?

- **Larry Flynt**

The will to persevere is often the difference between failure and success.

- David Sarnoff

Success is not in never failing, but rising every time you fall!

- Jonathan Taylor Thomas

Success is not to be pursued; it is to be attracted by the person you become.

- Jim Rohn

The talent of success is nothing more than doing what you can do well, and doing well whatever you do without thought of fame. If it comes at all it will come because it is deserved, not because it is sought after.

- Henry Wadsworth Longfellow

Success is about enjoying what you have and where you are, while pursuing achievable goals.

- Bo Bennett

We're born with success. It is only others who point out our failures, and what they attribute to us as failure.

- Whoopi Goldberg

I can give you a six-word formula for success: Think things through - then follow through.

- Eddie Rickenbacker

When someone asks, 'Does success make you into a monster?' I always say, 'No, it enables you to be a monster.'

- Simon Cowell

Ask any successful person to look back over the events of his or her life, and chances are there'll be a turning point of one kind or another. It doesn't matter if that success has come on a ball field or in a boardroom, in a research laboratory or on a campaign trail - it can usually be traced to some pivotal moment.

- Bill Rancic

The person who makes a success of living is the one who sees his goal steadily and aims for it unswervingly.

- Cecil B. DeMille

It doesn't matter whether you are pursuing success in business, sports, the arts, or life in general: The bridge between wishing and accomplishing is discipline.

- Harvey Mackay

Failure is not our only punishment for laziness; there is also the success of others.

- Jules Renard

The longer you hang in there, the greater the chance that something will happen in your favor. No matter how hard it seems, the longer you persist, the more likely your success.

- Jack Canfield

The superior man makes the difficulty to be overcome his first interest; success only comes later.

- Confucius

Without an open-minded mind, you can never be a great success.

- Martha Stewart

Most great people have attained their greatest success just one step beyond their greatest failure.

- Napoleon Hill

Always remember that striving and struggle precede success, even in the dictionary.

- Sarah Ban Breathnach

Think of yourself as on the threshold of unparalleled success. A whole, clear, glorious life lies before you. Achieve! Achieve!

- **Andrew Carnegie**

Just remember: to be grateful and thank the people who are there and support you along the way is a great start to success.

- **Meryl Davis**

Everything you need for better future and success has already been written. And guess what? All you have to do is go to the library.

- **Henri Frederic Amiel**

Whenever an individual or a business decides that success has been attained, progress stops.

- **Thomas J. Watson**

I think that my biggest attribute to any success that I have had is hard work. There really is no substitute for working hard.

- **Maria Bartiromo**

Sound character provides the power with which a person may ride the emergencies of life instead of being overwhelmed by them. Failure is... the highway to success.

- Og Mandino

I see my upbringing as a great success story. By disciplining me, my parents inculcated self-discipline. And by restricting my choices as a child, they gave me so many choices in my life as an adult. Because of what they did then, I get to do the work I love now.

- Amy Chua

If you create incredible value and information for others that can change their lives - and you always stay focused on that service - the financial success will follow.

- Brendon Burchard

People are the key to success or extraordinary success.

- Azim Premji

Success is nothing more than a few simple disciplines, practiced every day.

- Jim Rohn

Forward, as occasion offers. Never look round to see whether any shall note it... Be satisfied with success in even the smallest matter, and think that even such a result is no trifle.

- Marcus Aurelius

Success is the only motivational factor that a boy with character needs.

- Woody Hayes

Before everything else, getting ready is the secret of success.

- Henry Ford

Personal relationships are the fertile soil from which all advancement, all success, all achievement in real life grows.

- Ben Stein

Success can make you go one of two ways. It can make you a prima donna - or it can smooth the edges, take away the insecurities, let the nice things come out.

- Barbara Walters

Success requires first expending ten units of effort to produce one unit of results. Your momentum will then produce ten units of results with each unit of effort.

- Charles J. Givens

Never mind what others do; do better than yourself, beat your own record from day to day, and you are a success.

- William J. H. Boetcker

A man with a silver spoon may get his share of supporters, but he can never be an inspiration for somebody! Patience and hard work are the key to every man's success.

- Kailash Kher

Entrepreneurship is like a computer game in which you have to master every level before achieving success. Start-ups repeatedly stumble and have to go back to the drawing board. The best way to skip some levels and to increase the odds of survival is to learn from others who have already played the game.

- Vivek Wadhwa

Success is doing ordinary things extraordinarily well.

- Jim Rohn

No man ever achieved worthwhile success who did not, at one time or other; find himself with at least one foot hanging well over the brink of failure.

- Napoleon Hill

There's no abiding success without commitment.

- Tony Robbins

Achievement is not always success, while reputed failure often is. It is honest endeavor, persistent effort to do the best possible under any and all circumstances.

- Orison Swett Marden

When one side benefits more than the other, that's a win-lose situation. To the winner it might look like success for a while, but in the long run, it breeds resentment and distrust.

- Stephen Covey

While formal schooling is an important advantage, it is not a guarantee of success nor is its absence a fatal handicap.

- Ray Kroc

Women attribute their success to working hard, luck, and help from other people. Men will attribute that - whatever success they have, that same success - to their own core skills.

- Sheryl Sandberg

Success is attaining your dream while helping others to benefit from that dream materializing.

- Sugar Ray Leonard

The worst part of success is, to me, adapting to it. It's scary.

- Kendrick Lamar

Success is dependent upon the glands - sweat glands.

- Zig Ziglar

Success is the maximum utilization of the ability that you have.

- Zig Ziglar

It takes 20 years to make an overnight success.

- Eddie Cantor

We're constantly striving for success, fame and comfort when all we really need to be happy is someone or something to be enthusiastic about.

- H. Jackson Brown, Jr.

Men of age object too much, consult too long, adventure too little, repent too soon, and seldom drive business home to the full period, but content themselves with a mediocrity of success.

- Dale Carnegie

Men judge us by the success of our efforts. God looks at the efforts themselves.

- Charlotte Bronte

About the only problem with success is that it does not teach you how to deal with failure.

- Tommy Lasorda

Private dreams are the most powerful. You have to dream of success to make it happen, and if you don't believe in yourself, nobody else will. But that doesn't mean you have to go around telling everyone about it.

- Tony McCoy

I'll tell you, there is nothing better in life than being a late bloomer. I believe that success can happen at any time and at any age.

- **Salma Hayek**

I like people who are able to keep pushing themselves and challenging themselves even after great success.

- **John C. Reilly**

Success is a beast. And it actually puts the emphasis on the wrong thing. You get away with more instead of looking within.

- **Brad Pitt**

You've got to work hard for your success and you've got to have a steady presence. That's the secret.

- **Kid Rock**

Super-ambitious goals tend to be unifying and energizing to people; but only if they believe there's a chance of success.

- **Peter Diamandis**

Monetary success is not success. Career success is not success. Life, someone that loves you, giving to others, doing something that makes you feel complete and full. That is success. And it isn't dependent on anyone else.

- James Avery

When I think about parallels between myself and an Olympian, I believe that success in the world of business is underpinned by very similar principles of perseverance and hard work.

- Lakshmi Mittal

Success is almost totally dependent upon drive and persistence. The extra energy required to make another effort or try another approach is the secret of winning.

- Denis Waitley

Success isn't about the end result, it's about what you learn along the way.

- Vera Wang

You really have to work hard and apply yourself and by applying yourself and working hard and being diligent, you can achieve success.

- Julie Benz

Make treating yourself a priority and always remember your life is happening now. Don't put off all your dreams and pleasures to another day. In any balanced personal definition of success there has to be a powerful element of living life in the present.

- Mireille Guiliano

When I meet successful people I ask 100 questions as to what they attribute their success to. It is usually the same: persistence, hard work and hiring good people.

- Kiana Tom

Success usually comes to those who are too busy to be looking for it.

- Henry David Thoreau

Sound character provides the power with which a person may ride the emergencies of life instead of being overwhelmed by them. Failure is... the highway to success.

- Og Mandino

Raising children is an uncertain thing; success is reached only after a life of battle and worry.

- Democritus

Success is sweet and sweeter if long delayed and gotten through many struggles and defeats.

- Amos Bronson Alcott

The very first step towards success in any occupation is to become interested in it.

- William Osler

Your chances of success in any undertaking can always be measured by your belief in yourself.

- Robert Collier

Success in management requires learning as fast as the world is changing.

- Warren Bennis

People are the key to success or extraordinary success.

- Azim Premji

Fourth Law of Thermodynamics: If the probability of success is not almost one, then it is damn near zero.

- David R. Ellis

Success is the progressive realization of a worthy goal or ideal.

- Earl Nightingale

People seldom see the halting and painful steps by which the most insignificant success is achieved.

- Anne Sullivan

Success demands singleness of purpose.

- Vince Lombardi

Success comes when people act together; failure tends to happen alone.

- Deepak Chopra

Everyone who achieves success in a great venture, solves each problem as they came to it. They helped themselves. And they were helped through powers known and unknown to them at the time they set out on their voyage. They keep going regardless of the obstacles they met.

- W. Clement Stone

Perseverance - a lowly virtue whereby mediocrity achieves an inglorious success.

- Ambrose Bierce

How one handles success or failure is determined by their early childhood.

- Harold Ramis

All of us are born for a reason, but all of us don't discover why. Success in life has nothing to do with what you gain in life or accomplish for yourself. It's what you do for others.

- Danny Thomas

There's more to life than success, and if you can try to be more well-rounded, you'll be able to enjoy your success more. It won't own you or control you.

- Ricky Williams

Intuition is the wisdom formed by feeling and instinct - a gift of knowing without reasoning... Belief is ignited by hope and supported by facts and evidence - it builds alignment and creates confidence. Belief is what sets energy in motion and creates the success that breeds more success.

- Angela Ahrendts

You might well remember that nothing can bring you success but yourself.

- Napoleon Hill

You never achieve success unless you like what you are doing.

- Dale Carnegie

A constant struggle, a ceaseless battle to bring success from inhospitable surroundings, is the price of all great achievements.

- Orison Swett Marden

A desire to be in charge of our own lives, a need for control, is born in each of us. It is essential to our mental health, and our success, that we take control.

- Robert Foster Bennett

It's only lonely at the top if you forget all the people you met along the way and fail to acknowledge their contributions to your success.

- Harvey Mackay

Greater self-esteem produces greater success, and greater success produces more high self-esteem, so it keeps on spiralling up.

- Jack Canfield

Fact: From quitting smoking to skiing, we succeed to the degree we try, fail, and learn. Studies show that people who worry about mistakes shut down, but those who are relaxed about doing badly soon learn to do well. Success is built on failure.

- **Martha Beck**

I was happier when pursuing success than I was when savoring its fruits; the attraction, perhaps the addiction, was in the process, as much as in its end.

- **Michael Steinhardt**

True success has more components than one sentence or idea can contain.

- **Zig Ziglar**

Success must never be measured by how much money you have.

- **Zig Ziglar**

Time is the most precious element of human existence. The successful person knows how to put energy into time and how to draw success from time.

- **Denis Waitley**

The Lord gave us two ends - one to sit on and the other to think with. Success depends on which one we use the most.

- Ann Landers

The idea of capitalism is not just success but also the failure that allows success to happen.

- P. J. O'Rourke

An excuse becomes an obstacle in your journey to success when it is made in place of your best effort or when it is used as the object of the blame.

- Bo Bennett

You always pass failure on your way to success.

- Mickey Rooney

No man can be a failure if he thinks he's a success; If he thinks he is a winner, then he is.

- Robert W. Service

However things may seem, no evil thing is success and no good thing is failure.

- Henry Wadsworth Longfellow

In a person's career, well, if you're process-oriented and not totally outcome-oriented, then you're more likely to be a success. I often say 'pursue excellence, ignore success.' Success is a by-product of excellence.

- Deepak Chopra

If I had permitted my failures, or what seemed to me at the time a lack of success, to discourage me I cannot see any way in which I would ever have made progress.

- Calvin Coolidge

Anyone who wants to sell you overnight success or wealth is not interested in your success; they are interested in your money.

- Bo Bennett

The person interested in success has to learn to view failure as a healthy, inevitable part of the process of getting to the top.

- Joyce Brothers

People of mediocre ability sometimes achieve outstanding success because they don't know when to quit. Most men succeed because they are determined to.

- George Allen, Sr.

The first principle of success is desire - knowing what you want. Desire is the planting of your seed.

- Robert Collier

Whenever I've had success, I never learn from it. Success usually breeds a degree of hubris. When you fail, that's when you learn.

- Moby

Being happy is of the utmost importance. Success in anything is through happiness.

- Maharishi Mahesh Yogi

You've got to ask! Asking is, in my opinion, the world's most powerful - and neglected - secret to success and happiness.

- Percy Ross

I like people who are able to keep pushing themselves and challenging themselves even after great success.

- John C. Reilly

Philanthropy is the thing that I am really excited about, and having success means I can do more.

- will.i.am

There is no scientific answer for success. You can't define it. You've simply got to live it and do it.

- **Anita Roddick**

The lesson is, because there will be many lemons in life, to learn to make the proverbial lemonade - and be open and honest. That's the best way of doing damage control and positioning yourself for success.

- **Vivek Wadhwa**

In order that people may be happy in their work, these three things are needed: They must be fit for it. They must not do too much of it. And they must have a sense of success in it.

- **John Ruskin**

To have long term success as a coach or in any position of leadership, you have to be obsessed in some way.

- **Pat Riley**

No one can possibly achieve any real and lasting success or 'get rich' in business by being a conformist.

- **J. Paul Getty**

It is wise to keep in mind that neither success nor failure is ever final.

- Roger Babson

Earn your success based on service to others, not at the expense of others.

- H. Jackson Brown, Jr.

Ask yourself the secret of your success. Listen to your answer, and practice it.

- Richard Bach

Personal satisfaction is the most important ingredient of success.

- Denis Waitley

Success is not a stop sign.

- Robert Kiyosaki

I'd rather have huge success and huge failures than travel in the middle of the road.

- Kevyn Aucoin

When it comes to success, there are no shortcuts.

- Bo Bennett

Forget about the consequences of failure. Failure is only a temporary change in direction to set you straight for your next success.

- Denis Waitley

Honesty is the single most important factor having a direct bearing on the final success of an individual, corporation, or product.

- Ed McMahon

Real success is not on the stage, but off the stage as a human being, and how you get along with your fellow man.

- Sammy Davis, Jr.

Success is usually the culmination of controlling failure.

- Sylvester Stallone

Picture yourself vividly as winning, and that alone will contribute immeasurably to success.

- Harry Emerson Fosdick

Success is a journey, not a destination.

- Ben Sweetland

Success is more difficult to handle than failure.

- Ravi Zacharias

My success and my misfortunes, the bright and the dark days I have gone through, everything has proved to me that in this world, either physical or moral, good comes out of evil just as well as evil comes out of good.

- Giacomo Casanova

Positive thinking is the key to success in business, education, pro football, anything that you can mention. I go out there thinking that I'm going to complete every pass.

- Ron Jaworski

Success to me is being a good person, treating people well.

- David LaChapelle

Success is following the pattern of life one enjoys most.

- Al Capp

The key to accepting responsibility for your life is to accept the fact that your choices, every one of them, are leading you inexorably to either success or failure, however you define those terms.

- Neal Boortz

The secret to success is to own nothing, but control everything.

- Nelson Rockefeller

Success is not a place at which one arrives but rather the spirit with which one undertakes and continues the journey.

- Alex Noble

The only thing I have learnt over the years is that if you enjoy your work and put in the best efforts, it will show. If you follow this process, things work out. But if you go chasing a formula, success will elude you.

- Mahesh Babu

I don't really measure success by anything other than if I am happy. That is success to me. Am I happy waking up every morning? And despite the challenges of running my own business, do I look forward to going to work? Absolutely.

- L'Wren Scott

You do not pay the price of success, you enjoy the price of success.

- **Zig Ziglar**

One man cannot practice many arts with success.

- **Plato**

You know you are on the road to success if you would do your job, and not be paid for it.

- **Oprah Winfrey**

Our limitations and success will be based, most often, on your own expectations for ourselves. What the mind dwells upon, the body acts upon.

- **Denis Waitley**

In a lot of ways, success is much harder than I thought it would be. I figured that you'd get here and then everything would be happily ever after. But, it's hard work, almost harder once you're successful because you've got to maintain it.

- **Steven Wright**

The relationships we have with people are extremely important to success on and off the job.

- Zig Ziglar

I couldn't wait for success, so I went ahead without it.

- Jonathan Winters

The great secret of success is to go through life as a man who never gets used up.

- Albert Schweitzer

Success comes to those who have an entire mountain of gold that they continually mine, not those who find one nugget and try to live on it for fifty years.

- John C. Maxwell

I wonder how many times people give up just before a breakthrough - when they are on the very brink of success.

- Joyce Meyer

Success in any endeavor depends on the degree to which it is an expression of your true self.

- Ralph Marston

The secret of success in life is for a man to be ready for his opportunity when it comes.

- Benjamin Disraeli

Singleness of purpose is one of the chief essentials for success in life, no matter what may be one's aim.

- John D. Rockefeller

The envious man grows lean at the success of his neighbor.

- Horace

Success follows doing what you want to do. There is no other way to be successful.

- Malcolm Forbes

A minute's success pays the failure of years.

- Robert Browning

Temporary success can be achieved in spite of lack of other fundamental qualities, but no advancements can be maintained without hard work.

- William Feather

I cannot give you the formula for success, but I can give you the formula for failure - which is: Try to please everybody.

- Herbert Bayard Swope

Life affords no higher pleasure than that of surmounting difficulties, passing from one step of success to another, forming new wishes and seeing them gratified.

- Samuel Johnson

Entrepreneurs are risk takers, willing to roll the dice with their money or reputation on the line in support of an idea or enterprise. They willingly assume responsibility for the success or failure of a venture and are answerable for all its facets.

- Victor Kiam

To many a man, and sometimes to a youth, there comes the opportunity to choose between honorable competence and tainted wealth. The young man who starts out to be poor and honorable, holds in his hand one of the strongest elements of success.

- Orison Swett Marden

I believe there are three keys to success. For me it is keeping my priorities in order: It's my faith and my family, and then the business.

- **Kathy Ireland**

The power of fortune is confessed only by the miserable, for the happy impute all their success to prudence or merit.

- **Jonathan Swift**

I've learned that mistakes can often be as good a teacher as success.

- **Jack Welch**

The greatest thing a man can do in this world is to make the most possible out of the stuff that has been given him. This is success, and there is no other.

- **Orison Swett Marden**

Success is not in what you have, but who you are.

- **Bo Bennett**

You have reached the pinnacle of success as soon as you become uninterested in money, compliments, or publicity.

- **Thomas Wolfe**

Remember you will not always win. Some days, the most resourceful individual will taste defeat. But there is, in this case, always tomorrow - after you have done your best to achieve success today.

- **Maxwell Maltz**

Success is a consequence and must not be a goal.

- **Gustave Flaubert**

There is much to be said for failure. It is much more interesting than success.

- **Max Beerbohm**

I've known entrepreneurs who were not great salespeople, or didn't know how to code, or were not particularly charismatic leaders. But I don't know of any entrepreneurs who have achieved any level of success without persistence and determination.

- **Harvey Mackay**

The concept of the 'good ol' days' must be one of our society's biggest delusions, top reasons for depression, as well as most often used excuse for lack of success.

- **Bo Bennett**

The world judge of men by their ability in their profession, and we judge of ourselves by the same test: for it is on that on which our success in life depends.

- William Hazlitt

Humility is becoming a lost art, but it's not difficult to practice. It means that you realize that others have been involved in your success.

- Harvey Mackay

Enjoy your sweat because hard work doesn't guarantee success, but without it you don't have a chance.

- Alex Rodriguez

Success - it's what you do with what you've got.

- Woody Hayes

Being a part of success is more important than being personally indispensable.

- Pat Riley

I am fully aware that everybody has a right to succeed, and success should be with ethics.

- Sharad Pawar

With everything that is complex, we learn. If you don't learn, then it's an utter and abject failure. If you do learn, and you're able to apply that to the next situation, then you take away a measure of success.

- Benjamin Carson

I think you can have moderate success by copying something else, but if you really want to knock it out of the park, you have to do something different and take chances.

- Lee Ann Womack

No one ever attains success by simply doing what is required of him.

- Charles Kendall Adams

Money does not guarantee success.

- Jose Mourinho

Success cannot come from standstill men. Methods change and men must change with them.

- James Cash Penney

The secret of my success is that I make other people money. And, never ever, ever, ever be ashamed about trying to earn as much as possible for yourself, if the person you're working with is also making money. That's life!

- **Simon Cowell**

I've had a lot of success; I've had failures, so I learn from the failure.

- **Gordon Ramsay**

I have found no greater satisfaction than achieving success through honest dealing and strict adherence to the view that, for you to gain, those you deal with should gain as well.

- **Alan Greenspan**

Without failure there is no sweetness in success. There's no understanding of it.

- **Glenn Beck**

Success for me is to raise happy, healthy human beings.
- **Kelly LeBrock**

Get all of your failures out of the way quickly so you can start building up your successes.

- Robert Jamgotchian